A Geezer's Guide to the Universe

A Geezer's Guide to the Universe

Little Lessons from a Well-Lived Life

How You Can Find Opportunity, Satisfaction, Enjoyment, Love, and the Good Life Through Instinctive Thought and a Heartfelt Response

Real-life instructive stories that will inspire graduates and other first-time travelers on life's road

Dennis Glaser

Copyright © 2002 by Dennis Glaser.

Library of Congress Number: 2001119873
ISBN #: Hardcover 1-4010-4098-5
Softcover 1-4010-4097-7

All rights reserved. No part of this book may be reproduced or transmitted in any form or by any means, electronic or mechanical, including photocopying, recording, or by any information storage and retrieval system, without permission in writing from the copyright owner.

This book was printed in the United States of America.

To order additional copies of this book, contact:
Xlibris Corporation
1-888-7-XLIBRIS
www.Xlibris.com
Orders@Xlibris.com

Contents

My Rules 13
An Introduction 15
About This Book 17

LEARNING ON THE JOB

The Newspaper Years 23
Show Biz Was My Life! 47
Find a Job You Love and Never Work Again! 53
A Lesson in Power vs. Control 57
You Have to Take a Stand Sometimes 59
First, Make a Good Impression 63
Sow's Ears and Silk Purses 67

LIVE WELL

More Work Than Working 75
Greed Is Its Own Reward 77
It's Hard to be a Christian Soldier 81

LAUGH OFTEN

My Brief Career As a 'Cycle-Riding Bootlegger 85
The Great Watermelon Raid 89
Climbing Social Ladders and Falling Down Stairs 93
No Laws Against Laughter or Stupidity 97
Going Out of My Head at Mardi Gras 101
The Mazda and the Mechanic 103

LOVE MUCH

The Mother's Heart Is the Child's Schoolroom 107
Things I Learned From My Father 109
Memories of Christmases Past 113
Pick Your Parking Place With Care 115
I Never Forget a Face!
  (Now, What Was Your Name Again?) 117
You Gotta Pay the Piper—and the Judge, too! 119
One in Time Can Last for Nine! 121
The 'Capitol' Girl of the North Atlantic 123
The Gold-Digger Problem 127
A Martyr to Safe Sex? 129

BEST FRIENDS

A Gift of Love from My Dog Freckles 135
Freedom: Not Just Another Word to a Parrot 141
Snakes, Kittens & Puppy Dogs 151

On My Own with a Wife, a Child, and a St. Bernard 155
Me and Wildlife 159

LESSONS TAUGHT BY NATURE

Why I Moved to the Country 165
The Nature of Nature 171
Nature's Law of Compensation 177
Gardening on the Right Side of the Brain 181
Spring Comes to Tennessee 187
Things You Might Learn From Nature 189
Lonesome Is As Lonesome Does 193
Life As a Lad in the 'Good Old Days' 197
Me and My Chainsaw 201
Self-Reliance; Not Self-Sufficiency 205
An Almost True Story 209
Night Sounds in the Country 211

ON THE ROAD AGAIN

A Stranger in a Strange Land 215
Life in a Small French Village 217
I Have Met the Universe, and It Is Us 219
An Afterword 225

To all the women I've loved before, and to the many I still loved after, I dedicate this book.

And especially to those who really, really did love me.
In the words of the master, William Shakespeare:
Ophelia: 'Tis brief, my lord.
Hamlet: As woman's love.

> Whatever you do, you need courage. Whatever course you decide upon, there is always some one to tell you you are wrong. There are always difficulties arising which tempt you to believe that your critics are right. To map out a course of action and follow it to the end, requires some of the same courage which a soldier needs. Peace has its victories, but it takes brave men to win them.

—Ralph Waldo Emerson

My Rules

- You always should be prepared to pay for your thrills.

- No one wants to buy you a drink when you are sober, but everyone wants to buy you one when you are already drunk.

- You create your own reality: It is not what happens, but how you view it.

- If it is not your own belief, then you don't actually believe it.

- Would you rather be right or would you rather experience peace?

An Introduction

This is a non-fiction book. Most of the essays or stories are brief, so it might be a book that you will sample from time to time, rather than read it straight through, from beginning to end.

Most of it is autobiographical in nature. The experiences and observations are my own, unless specifically noted otherwise. I hope you enjoy reading it as much as I enjoyed living it, and then writing it.

About This Book

I was first encouraged by my friend in France, Chantal Chorfi, to compile these little stories of incidents from my life. Possibly she was acting in self-defense—wearying of hearing me spin them out for her and probably now and then hearing me tell her the same story twice. So I began putting the "stories of my life" into the written word. At first, I viewed the exercise as possibly leading to magazine articles, since a part of my journalism years were spent as a magazine staff writer/editor.

But, as my computer files grew, I realized that: 1) I had the makings of a book, and 2) although I have lived in times vastly different from those that most young people must meet and master today, many of the basic truths that I had discovered from my life might be of some value to those who are leaving home and school and venturing forth into what some of us call "the real world."

My own experience in the workaday world has included: newspaper reporter, then editor; newspaper ad salesman, then ad sales manager; purchase of a small daily newspaper which I then expanded to include eight community newspapers and a web offset printing center; music business personal manager, then writer/editor of a music fan magazine, music public relations, president/owner of a small record/tape manufacturing plant; advertising copywriter, then mid-level ad department management; and finally, freelance writer. And now: my first published book.

If this were a speech written for an Oscar winner, I would want to say that I owe my thanks to many other people. Some because of their critical appraisals of my work only inspired me to continue to put more words on paper but to do it better. And others because their words of encouragement and appreciation for my efforts encouraged me to push harder, accomplish more, and do the physical work that goes with spending hours and hours in front of a computer screen; writing and re-writing, editing, organizing, and always pushing on toward the day when the presses would begin to roll.

So, to Martha, Roger, Ruthie, Cheryl, Sarah, Lori, Chantal, Danyele, Kent, Eve, Roy, Denise, Hope, Sherrie, Cloe, Linda Sue, Kathy, Jane, Sibylle, Deb, Hope, Randy, Teresa, Naomi, Diana, Mary Kaye, Captain Midnite, Judy, Angela, Eleana, and all the rest of my friends and relatives: You know who you are. Thank you. If you like what I've written, please buy a copy or two for your young friends who might benefit from something in the book. If you don't like it, please keep your opinions to yourself!

And to the younger generation to whom I address these little pieces of the puzzle that my life has been, I suggest that you consider these stories not as hard and fast rules for living your life, but rather as examples of what one of your predecessors saw, heard, and did. Your experiences in this 21st century and a new millennium will of course differ greatly from mine as I labored in the 20th century vineyards. But it is my hope that these glimpses of my pathway may provide some examples for you— examples to follow or to avoid. As you will.

And to those of my golden oldies or "geezer" generation: Please turn to your special invitation at the end of this book.

Dennis Glaser
Rossville, Georgia;
Nashville, Tennessee, and
Fontaine sous Ouerre, France
June 2001

Geezer Glimpses

The meeting of two personalities is like the contact of two chemical substances; if there is any reaction, both are transformed, said Carl Jung

Thus I believe love is a force that changes our individual experience from particle to wave; from separate "stuff" to connected energy. As two people join forces, they also combine their energy. You can see that in action by noting the wave caused when you toss a stone into a pond. When two stones are tossed at the same time, the two waves of energy combine into one.

Too often we are "searching for the right person instead of trying to be the right person."

"When one is in love, one always begins by deceiving oneself, and one always ends by deceiving others. That is what the world calls romance."—Oscar Wilde: *The Picture of Dorian Gray IV*

"The real way of living is to answer to one's wants, not 'I want to light up with my intelligence as many things as possible,' but 'I want that pound of peaches' . . . 'I want to kiss that girl' . . . 'I want to insult that man.'"—D. H. Lawrence, quoted in W. D. Snodgrass, *In Radical Pursuit.*

"I gave sugar for sugar
Now I give salt for salt.
You don't like it, baby,
And I guess it's your own goddamned fault."
—Traditional blues song

Geezer Gatherings

Maurice Ravel is popularly known as the composer of Ravel's Bolero, although his later fame far exceeded that simplistic effort. About him one reviewer wrote: "If Ravel seemed cold and aloof as a man, it must have been not because he felt too little, but because he felt too much."

Ravel himself once wrote:

"[An artist] must be very careful when he wishes to marry someone, because an artist never knows to what extent he may render his companion unhappy. He is obsessed by his creative work and by the problems which it poses. He lives a little like an awakened dreamer, and that's not amusing for a woman who lives with him. One must always consider that when one wishes to marry."

Yes. After my own three marriages, I do know what he meant!

"But if he could describe it all
He would be an artist.
But if he were an artist there would be deeper wounds
Which he could not describe."
    Edgar Lee Masters: *Silence*, from *Songs and Satires*

LEARNING ON THE JOB

> " A man should feel confident concerning his soul, who has renounced those pleasures and fineries that go with the body, as being alien to him . . . but has pursued the pleasures that go with learning. . . . "

Socrates: 469-399 B.C.

Geezer Grumblings

I love my country, but that doesn't mean I can overlook some things that are wrong with our way of life. Here's a few examples:

Why should the U.S. take the responsibility for policing the world? Our political and economic leaders use words like "our way of life," and "free trade" and "protecting human rights." But, to the rest of the world, it appears that our economic leaders are using military power to impose our culture on the rest of the world. And they would define "culture" as "buying stuff from America." Maybe we should realize that, while we like the way we live in the United States, perhaps people living in other countries, on other continents, would prefer to hold onto their own cultures instead of being force-fed our way of doing things.

Much of our military budget goes to insure our access to overseas oil-producing nations. Yet, we know that continuing to power our lifestyle with fossil fuels is degrading the earth's ecology. The major oil companies are not U.S.-owned anymore. We have the technology to generate electric power from the sun—one hour of sunlight could produce enough electricity for the entire world! One year's defense budget would go far to pay for the change.

Here at home, we spend enormous sums on highways and cars and trucks. The same investment could provide highspeed rail transportation powered by electricity to serve every corner of the country, using small cars only for local travel. And most trucks would be gone from our highways.

Yes, it would mean the end of the industries that now sell us highway construction and cars and trucks and gas and oil. But this kind of change has happened before. A century ago, we changed from horsepower to oil power. Maybe it is time—past time—for another giant step forward into the future.

And through it all, I stood tall, And did it my way!
—From the song, *My Way*, as sung by Frank Sinatra and others

The Newspaper Years

It all started when I was in grade school, at Pibel District No. 9, in Wheeler County, Nebraska. One of us brothers received a toy typewriter for Christmas. In my mind, it was mine. But my older brother Harold always maintained it was his—and maybe it was. I don't remember ever seeing him use it—and I know that I did. Because it was with this little toy typewriter that one summer I published copies of the *Pibel News*.

It was slow work. For each letter of every word, you had to turn a disk by hand to the letter you wanted, and then push down the lever which brought the raised letter into contact with the paper. There must have been a ribbon involved, or some kind of inking mechanism. We'll never know, because Harold stored the typewriter in the basement of my newspaper plant while he was working for me . . . and somebody stole it.

As I remember, I made an original and a couple of carbon copies of what I considered to be "news" on a 8 1/2 x 11-inch page—two columns to a page, and probably no more than one page per issue. For a time, I distributed it by putting a copy in each of the 4 or 5 mailboxes that were mounted on an old wagon wheel to serve us and our neighbors at the end of Rural Route 1, Spalding, Nebr.

But then the mail carrier—John Kinnear—found me waiting for the mail one day and told me that it was a violation of federal law to put anything in the mailbox except actual postage-paid U.S. mail! So I stopped. But I also stopped putting apples for him in our mailbox since I couldn't figure out how to attach a postage stamp to an apple.

I used to ride my horse to the mile-distant mailbox each day. Once a new tire my father had ordered from the Sears mail-order catalog came in the mail. How to carry it home? Easy. I hung it around the horse's neck. One of our neighbors saw me thus, and telephoned my mother to tell me how funny it looked!

When I was a sophomore in high school, I applied for a chance to work at the shop of the *Spalding Enterprise* weekly newspaper. The editor and publisher, Don Bopp, said he couldn't afford to hire anyone, but if I wanted to come in after school, he'd give me a chance to learn the layout of letters in the hand-set type drawer by putting the letters from the display headlines back into the proper place in the right drawer after the paper was printed. And, later, he even let me run the Linotype machine! But when he told me to sweep the floor, I pointed out that I already knew how to use a broom, so I felt I should be paid for doing that. And he did pay me; probably 5 or 10 cents an hour.

Wednesday was press day, and we printed two pages at a time, working most of the night. The press was powered by a gasoline engine. Usually four of the eight pages of each issue were Western Newspaper Union readyprint—I think the deal was you got the newsprint free but WNU filled one side of each sheet with preprinted general information articles and advertisements, of course.

One benefit of the job was it gave me the chance to buy beer. Don Bopp liked a bottle or more during those late-night printing sessions, and would send me to a nearby bar to buy a six-pack for him. So, of course, when I wanted to buy some for myself and my friends, how was the bartender to know it wasn't for Editor Bopp? The Bopp family, by the way, still publishes the paper and, until a few years ago, it still was produced and printed by letterpress. Maybe one of the last in the country since photo offset came into popularity.

The next time I remember even thinking about journalism as

a career was while I was in Coast Guard radio operator's school in Atlantic City, N. J., and the atom bomb brought a sudden and welcome end to World War II. I realized that I'd be going back to civilian life one day (actually, it didn't happen until the following June, 1946). And I began wondering what I would do with the rest of my life. The war had started in 1939 so all during my adolescence and youthful years, I'd never known anything else.

I knew that I liked to write. Even before I started to high school, I wrote a poem about how unions should support the war effort by banning labor strikes and took it to the Spalding paper to be published. The "hook" was something to the effect that "instead of bars and strikes, it should be stars and stripes" that working men ought to be thinking about. I was a budding Republican in those days: I wrote to the Wendell Wilkie presidential campaign office in Omaha to offer my support, and they sent me a supply of campaign signs and stickers. I was 12 years old at the time.

When I was stationed in Newfoundland, one of the other men there was from Boulder, Colorado, and he urged me to attend college at the University of Colorado in that city. They had a great journalism department, he said.

But a funny thing happened to me on the way to college. I spent that first summer after my discharge at home, painting the family house which was in need of a new coat. One day, I had a bad stomach ache. After a day of it, my mother gave me some laxative—not a good idea. Because the pain got even worse, so they took me to a doctor in Spalding, who diagnosed it as appendicitis and sent me on to Grand Island's hospital. No VA hospitals had been built yet, so there went my savings!

Geezer Gleanings

From *A Curmudgeon's Garden of Love*:

Henny Youngman: Why do Jewish divorces cost so much? Because they're worth it.

Erica Jong: Beware of the man who praises women's liberation; he is about to quit his job.

Jules Renard: Love is like an hourglass, with the heart filling up as the brain empties.

Mort Sahl: We would have broken up except for the children. Who were the children? Well, she and I were.

Eric Berne: No man is a hero to his wife's psychiatrist.

Alexander Woollcott: Nothing risqué, nothing gained.

Geoffrey Gorer: The trouble with my wife is that she is a whore in the kitchen and a cook in bed.

I remember nothing about the pre-operation procedures. Probably I was too sick to pay much attention. But when I regained consciousness, I was in a room with another young guy who also had undergone the same operation. His doctor was an old man; mine was a young man just out of the Army and trained on the newest procedures. The other patient and I compared scars: Mine was very small, while his was about 6 inches long. His doctor let him drink water right away; mine would only permit me to suck on a piece of ice, but I couldn't swallow the water, he said.

I was out of the hospital in 3 or 4 days, but the other guy was still there. Then I read in the paper that he had died! I should have realized then that I would have a charmed life. The gods smiled on me and assigned the young Army-trained surgeon to my case.

As I've related elsewhere, more good fortune came when I narrowly escaped a dead-end career as a railroad telegrapher by meeting a woman whose husband was an instructor in the very school I'd planned to enroll in on the G.I. Bill. Instead, she suggested I attend Omaha Tech where her daughter was a student, as it had a great journalism sequence, including a printing shop.

I became an editor of the school paper and, after one semester, was offered my first newspaper job at the Manhattan (Kansas) *Tribune-News* by Al Horlings, who had been a journalism instructor at Kansas State College. Within 2 or 3 years, I was successively police beat and court house reporter, farm editor, advertising manager, and managing editor of his weekly newspapers.

But I wanted to own my own! Newly married and now with a daughter to raise, I heard about this guy Huck Boyd in Phillipsburg, Kansas, who liked to hire ambitious young men, work 'em hard, and then help them buy their own papers. Usually he had picked college graduates, but I guess he saw something in me—I must have been about 21 or 22—and hired me. Huck went on to become national Republican committeeman from Kansas and played an important role in the election of Eisenhower as president.

I learned a lot from Huck, but finally realized that his political career had sapped his financial ability to underwrite my newspaper purchase. So, when Horlings asked me to come back to Manhattan, I did. On the basis that I would eventually buy his newspaper operation and meantime I would accumulate the money to pay for it from my salary plus a 50% share of the profits. He'd gone to daily publication during the interim, failed, and had now published two weeklies plus a monthly magazine, *Land Improvement*, which was edited for soil conservation contractors. He would retain the magazine, but in the meantime, I would be associate publisher of it also. And we started a new farm newspaper, *Grass & Grain*. Radically for its time, *Grass & Grain* was free circulation, distributed to about 25 thousand homes by U.S. Mail, addressed to rural route boxholders. One of the other weeklies was the original *Tribune-News*, now a shadow of its former self, and the *Fort Riley Guidon*, published for the nearby Army post.

At the end of the first year, I discovered that my share of the profits would be much smaller than the monthly Profit & Loss reports had indicated. Al explained that he had bought a carload of newsprint in December—which we didn't yet need—as a tax avoidance move. I took it as handwriting on the wall—and started looking for a paper to buy on my own.

I found one in Missouri, but the town was too small and the price too high. Then I saw an ad offering *The Lewistown (Illinois) Daily News* on terms that I thought I could handle. After considerable correspondence and a weekend visit, we signed the contract papers and took over.

The owner had lied and misled me on many points. I knew what I was up against when the paychecks he had written to the employees for his last week all bounced! Of course, I made the checks good. Then I found out that a local car dealer had a second mortgage on the place, which I had unwittingly assumed through a bit of legal mumbo-jumbo. But one of the local banks loaned me a few thousand dollars to pay him off and to keep us going, and we struggled to solvency through a lot of long hours, hard work, and the knowledge that 10 cents worth of spending was equal to at least a dollar's worth of sales. So, of course, the best way to "make money" was to avoid spending it!

First, I'll itemize the various stages the business went through, and then recall some of the crucial decisions that were involved along the way.

The Lewistown Daily News. When I took over—I think it was Labor Day weekend of 1958—the paper was being printed 50 miles away at Washington, Illinois, in the plant of the weekly but better equipped *Reporter* newspaper. As part of the quid pro quo, my Model 14 Linotype was in Washington, Illinois, and their Heidelberg job press was in Lewistown. In theory, I was to do their commercial printing to partially offset the cost of the newspaper production. But not by much. I hired one of their printers, who lived in Lewistown, to run the press for me on Saturdays.

We had an INS teletype for national and world news (INS later merged with United Press to become UPI, and eventually was overtaken and subdued by the Associated Press). Norma Chambers, one of my employees, would drive to Washington each morning with the day's news and ad copy, leaving about 6 a.m. So I'd get up at 5, and edit the teletype national and international copy, putting the stories in order by priority since there was no way to know how much space I'd have to fill that day. Then, at 11 a.m., we had an open phone line to the *Reporter* so we could dictate late local or national news. Norma would be back before school was out with the printed copies so the newsboys could distribute them to our local subscribers. Deciding several hours ahead of the time when subscribers would read the paper just what should be my leading non-local news story was difficult. Until one morning

I was up early and stopped at a coffee shop for breakfast. Listening to what other customers were talking about after reading the Peoria morning daily gave me a good clue, and usually I made the right choice.

It was not a good arrangement, but it did give me six months (the longest period I would agree to upfront) to master the other phases of the business. Since the Wednesday paper was our biggest, ad-wise, and since we also competed locally with both a mimeographed free shopper publication and a small weekly newspaper, the *Daily News* also published a free-circulation throwaway on Wednesday, which contained the grocery store ads and so on. The other four days of the week, the paper was usually only four or six pages.

About the time the six months were up, the county Farm Bureau invited me to submit a bid on printing their monthly newsletter that they sent to their 3,000 members all over Fulton County (which had a total population of about 40,000 people). *The News'* circulation was under 2,000, with another couple of thousand copies of the free paper on Wednesday.

I saw an opportunity. The newsletter was costing the Farm Bureau about $5000 a year to print and mail. So I asked to meet with their board of directors and presented my alternative. For $1 a year per member, they would receive a subscription to the Wednesday issue of *The News*. And each of those issues would include a half-page of Farm Bureau news and advertising by their companies. To this I would add another half-page of county farm extension news, so there'd be a full page of farm news.

I checked it with the post office, and it was legal. The Farm Bureau's membership receipt included a statement that $1 of the annual membership fee was for a subscription which allowed me to mail the papers at the then cheaper second class postage rates. My competing newspaper sent a lawyer to Washington, D.C., to contest it, but I appealed for help from the powerful state Farm Bureau, and they put their national organization's legal eagles on the case—and I won.

Geezer Guidelines

Does it feel like the pressure is on? I think it was songwriter Joe South who said that when we're born, someone straps a pack on our back and tells us we have to have it full before we die. For an alternative view, read below what Ralph Waldo Emerson had to say about success, and the way in which he said it:

To laugh often and love much;
to win the respect of intelligent persons and the affection of children;
to earn the approbation of honest critics and to endure the betrayal of
    false friends;
to appreciate beauty;
to find the best in others;
to give of one's self;
to leave the world a bit better, whether by a healthy child, a garden
    patch, or a redeemed social condition;
to have played and laughed with enthusiasm and sung with exultation;
to know that even one life has breathed easier because you have lived—
    this is to have succeeded.

My newspaper competitor in Lewistown—the *Fulton Democrat*—tossed another "bouquet" my way when I suspended publication for one day while the equipment was being moved back to my printing plant. They cited the fact that failing to print for one day made my newspaper ineligible for publishing legal notices for six months! Gee, I wish I would have known about that—for I could easily have published a one-page issue in advance and called it the Friday paper.

But, I survived without the legals—I wasn't getting many of them anyway. My paper had a history of frequent bankruptcies in its brief prior history, I wasn't the butt-kissing type the local lawyers seemed to prefer, and my competitor was the son of the man who had published the paper back as many years as one could easily contemplate. Plus he was a political activist, hung out at a local bar, and everybody in town was about half afraid of what he might print about them if they crossed his path.

At any rate, now I had the largest circulation of any newspaper in the county, other than the six-day daily in the county's "big" city of Canton, which claimed about 10,000 copies, I think.

The Cuba Journal. One of my grocery advertisers had stores in both Lewistown and Cuba, and insisted on full-coverage (via the free paper) in the city of Cuba. The weekly there was owned by the local superintendent of the city schools. He worked on the paper nights and Saturdays and employed a woman Linotype operator fulltime. He suggested that I take over publication until his retirement and I agreed. Unfortunately, our agreement was verbal and eventually wound up in court, although we always intended to put it into a legal contract.

So, with another 1,000 paid circulation, and a bit more advertising revenue, I decided to change to a tri-weekly, publishing The News on Monday, Wednesday and Friday, and *The Journal* on Wednesday. We dropped the free-circulation paper much of the time, using instead our legal privilege of distributing 10% of our circulation to non-subscribers at the less expensive second class postage rates.

Goodyear Tire Company. One day, a Goodyear farm tire salesman came into my office, having been directed there by Harold Hyzer, whose house I had recently purchased, and who was the local Goodyear dealer. The Goodyear guy had been transferred to Illinois from another state where he'd promoted a farm tire circular advertising program. It worked like this. The printer (me) would design a four-page newspaper-sized circular for his approval, and print 500 or 1000 copies. The salesman would show the circular to his retail dealers with the proposal that if they bought x-number of tires, they would have x-number of circulars mailed to local rural route boxholders at a cost of 5 cents each, including about 3.5 cents postage. Payable in advance to me.

The salesman would then send me the check, a list of the rural routes and the number on each route, the dealer's signature copy, and the date he wanted the handbills delivered. We would print and mail them, having notified the postmasters involved when to expect the shipment and the dates the dealer had requested for delivery. And, as it turned out, the circulars were very successful in selling tires.

I had two high school boys working for me then, plus a deaf man who was the Linotype operator, but who couldn't do anything else in the plant. So whenever the press wasn't being used to produce the newspaper, we'd print Goodyear circulars. The press had to be fed by hand, one big four-page sheet at a time, and then the printed sheets were handfed again through the folding machine. Then counted, bundled and labeled, and sacked in labeled mailbags.

That first time, working with only the one salesman's territory, I think we printed and mailed about 60,000 copies, with a profit of roughly 1 cent each, or $600. But it sold tires! And now the company wanted to extend it to the entire state of Illinois—and do it twice a year!

Timing, they say, is everything. Woody Allen put it best: Success is 95% just showing up. Whatever. I prefer to think that the gods were again smiling on me. "Look how hard that guy is trying," they said. "Let's give him a break." Web offset was the answer, and my savior.

I knew all about web offset, having read every printing trade magazine I could lay my hands on, and was convinced that it was the coming thing. Offset is a photographic reproduction process that does not require metal type, which has to be set on a machine operated by a skilled typesetter. With an offset press, all you do is produce one copy, by any means, photograph it on a page-size camera, and use the resulting film to make an aluminum plate from which thousands of paper reproductions can be printed at very high speeds from a roll or "web" of paper. And folded in the same operation.

I didn't have one, and couldn't afford to buy a web offset press, but I wanted one. Fortunately, the newspaper at Morton, Illinois—like Washington, a suburb of Peoria—installed one. And they were looking for work to keep that press busy. So, I converted my newspapers to offset, at first continuing to set type in hot metal, but soon switching to IBM typewriters with proportionally spaced letters which allowed us to typeset in even columns by typing every line twice. But still faster and cheaper than Linotype work. Women who could type were easier to find than trained printers were. In fact, it didn't take me long to realize that women were better workers; I even hired one to run the smaller commercial printing presses. Give a woman a promotion, and she works even harder. Men? Well, too often they would think they'd been promoted for what they knew instead of what they could do!

And I switched Lewistown from three papers a week to just one, on Wednesday. And renamed it *The Fulton County News*, to reflect our wider readership. A local attorney stopped in at the office late one afternoon, and I told him of my hopes and, really, dreams. He had a proposal. We could buy a much larger building than the one we were renting, and buy a press. He would put up the cash we needed and, as a board member of the Savings &

Loan, help us get the additional financing we'd need to remodel the vacant building, etc.

The press—I started with one unit which would print 4 pages at one time at a speed of 20,000 an hour—would cost about $35,000. But I could lease it, which required a smaller down payment. And the lawyer would take a 25% interest in the business, which we incorporated under the name of Mid-County Press.

Good thing I'd decided to expand, because when my Goodyear guy, who lived in Morton, stopped at the newspaper office there to buy some layout sheets, they told him, hey, why bother going through Glaser since we're doing his printing anyway? Fortunately for me, the tire man was the kind of guy who didn't like unethical people and immediately told me all about it. And told me that I still had his business, which, by the way, was going to be expanded to include parts of adjoining states.

So it was that one day, the vice-president in charge of purchasing for all Goodyear operations in the United States called and said he was coming to Lewistown to get acquainted. It seems that they might also give us the printing of special one-store promotional advertising for their company-owned retail stores all over the country.

But it was too soon! I was still in the old building, and my printing plant was filled with no-longer-used equipment since the new press was still in the future. At first, I figured I'd have to fake it: tell him that insurance regulations didn't permit visitors to enter the printing department. But when he arrived, I could sense an instant rapport, so I told him the truth—and he believed me.

I hired a local contractor I'd come to know well through the American Legion. George Gray had been wounded in the war, and walked with a limp and had a steel plate in his skull. But he was the best contractor I've ever known. He handled the major stuff, and I did the interior painting myself, and took his advice and lowered the ceilings by running 2x4's across, and laying wallboard sheets on top of them.

Geezer Gifts

Most people don't really get interested in local politics until they get arrested.

People who always say they have no friends always say it to their friends.

When pride is all he has left, a man will either give it up willingly or not at all.

No one will buy you a drink when you're sober but everyone wants to buy you one when you're drunk.

People with time to kill always want to do it with people who don't have time to kill.

Observation resulting from one visit to a singles bar: The man who lives by the check will never lack for sex.

"Yeah, I'm going to have surgery. Gonna have my fibroids, thyroids, hemorrhoids, and paranoids removed."

Sin seems to be more a matter of opportunity than of inclination.

But he misjudged what the weight of the press would do the floor of the pressroom. It sagged. So, late one night, we propped it up with cement blocks that I put into position myself as I didn't want anyone else to take the risk of having a several-ton press dropping atop them! Later, George cut holes in the floor and poured concrete pillars for added strength, and we then moved the press back atop the pillars.

Things happened fast after then, and I don't remember clearly in what order all of the following took place.

Goodrich Tire Co. One day, a man showed up in our new offices, clutching a copy of a Goodyear Tire circular. "Are you the farm tire handbill king?" he asked. I said, yes, I guess I was. He'd tracked me down by the postage permit, which included "Lewistown, IL." and asked the local post office who owned that permit. (The post office, by the way, had already grown from a "third class" office to "first class" based on the increase in postage payments—which also increased the salary of the postmaster. So I could count on his cooperation—even to the point of occasionally holding up a mail truck for a shipment of circulars that just had to go out that night.)

Goodrich wanted the same deal, and my word that I would maintain client confidentiality—that I wouldn't tell Goodyear what Goodrich was up to, and of course, I assured Goodyear of the same protection. Well, the upshot was that Goodrich gave us the entire United States! I don't recall how many copies we printed—hundreds of thousands twice a year. But I do remember that never once did we mail the wrong order to the wrong towns and never did we have a complaint of a missed deadline. To make sure that the pressman would print the right number of copies, I included a code with the store's name and address that included the number needed and the mailing date.

And we hired women to work part-time as needed to bundle, tie and bag the printed copies. And bought an automatic bundle tying machine. And set up a gravity-fed conveyor system so the women worked in a room separate from the pressroom. And began buying newsprint by the carload. And gained the local American Legion's permission to buy a slice of their lot next door to us so I could have additional warehouse space built for newsprint storage—which, up to that time, we stored on the second floor, moving it up and down on an old freight elevator.

Ah, it was fun while it lasted! But all good things come to an end. A printer in Iowa underbid us for the Goodyear job. And the Goodrich vice president retired. His successor had a relative in Omaha who just happened to also have a web offset press!

But, meanwhile, other things were happening that eventually filled the gap that was left when we lost that income.

Competition. Ken Stevens, who had worked for the Ord (Nebraska) *Quiz*, bought the small weekly at Astoria, not far from Lewistown. Full of big ideas, he thought we should own the web press together. OK, I said, and we'll put it half-way between Astoria and Lewistown. No, in Astoria, he said. The difference between us was he liked to own what he saw, and I just liked to do community journalism. To me, a new press was a means to the end. To him, it was the end—and he'd use any means to get to it.

In Havana, just across the Illinois river from me, Bob Martin was publishing a small shopper on a sheetfed offset press. I of course wanted his business. He suggested a trade: I could use his pressman and print his papers (his and another shopper at Farmington) for him, with him paying only for the paper. I decided to go for it, although I knew that he was some kind of shirt-tail relation to the wife of Gilman Davidson, publisher of the *Fulton Democrat*, my direct newspaper competitor.

Big mistake. What Martin did was order his own web press—without telling me until the week it arrived. Fortunately, one of my own men—Roger Hagaman—and I had learned enough about the press to survive. Much later, when Davidson died or retired, Martin got the *Democrat* and, through some other skulduggery, also wound up buying his competition in Havana. In that case, the father sold the paper out from under the nose of his own son, who was part-owner. So much for ethics.

Somewhere about this time, I was doing so much printing that I decided to add a second 4-page press unit. Gary Hansen, the Wisconsin man who installed it for the manufacturer, liked me and small town life and hit me up for a job. I hired him, and later found out that he really didn't know as much about the printing process as he had led me to believe—but he was a quick learner.

The Washington Courier. One of my printing customers was the competitor to the *Washington Reporter*, the newspaper where I originally had the *News* printed those first six months. The *Courier*'s owner, a man named Paul Van Stavern (everyone called him Van), was getting old, and not making any money. He wanted to sell, but couldn't bring himself to the point of actually agreeing to a deal.

After we'd met two or three times with his attorney—a man named Heiple whose son later ran for and was elected to the state legislature with a lot of help from me—the attorney called and asked me to meet with him alone. And the lawyer wanted to know what I was willing to pay. I outlined the deal I was prepared to accept, and he then convinced Van Stavern to make the sale.

About that same time, I started printing the *Creve Coeur Shopper*, which was owned by a local grocer in that Peoria suburb who needed it to get full coverage for his own ad. But he sold ads to others also—including other grocers! He started a second shopper in Morton, competing with the paper where I had my offset work done before buying my own press.

A guy named Marvin did the production work on the Morton project; maybe the Creve Coeur one too, I don't remember. Anyway, he hired an ad salesman named Roger Hagel, just out of the Air Force and home from the Korean War. Somehow—and I don't remember exactly how it worked—I wound up with the *Morton Shopper*. Roger was the man I needed to manage the more prosperous Washington operation, and I hired another promoter-type named Wilf to run the Morton office.

Wilf always wanted to "talk things over" with me, and frequently would show up unannounced in Lewistown on Saturday when we were trying to get some work done. I certainly remember the time he arrived and I hid in a storeroom until he finally gave up and left. Eventually, I sold the Morton paper to him, and later, after I sold the *Courier* to Roger, Roger also bought the Morton paper.

The Spring Valley Gazette. During the Goldwater-Johnson election, a young Republican activist named Tom McMurray came to me for a bid on printing huge quantities of a four-page tabloid which compared the records of the two candidates. Tom had been an assistant to Bob Michel, the longtime U.S. congressman from Peoria—and Tom's ambition was to run for that office when Michel stepped down.

Tom was a Catholic from Peoria, with a big family. So big that, on the salary I paid him (yes, he came to work for me) he qualified for food stamps! He tried to get the job of printing the Catholic diocese newspaper for us, but it would have involved providing office space for some priests every week. He did get us the job of printing the national Young Republican newspaper monthly.

The Spring Valley Gazette. Tom wanted a base of operations in Michel's district, and we came across a newspaper for sale in Spring Valley, about 50 miles north of Peoria. It was owned by a local man there who was in the road construction business. Wise to the ways of state politics, he was said to have figured he could use the newspaper to obtain some lucrative state printing though his connections in Springfield, or so I was told. Well, there was a big scandal about this sort of thing, and his plans fell through. The newspaper was in technical bankruptcy—it was incorporated. So I bought it, after some hard negotiations. And immediately sold the equipment, etc., and moved the printing to Lewistown.

It never made much money, if any. At one point, a new factory was being built in nearby Hennipin, so we started a shopper for that town, which had no newspaper. But the factory didn't bring the influx of people that had been expected, so we killed it off a few months later, as I explain below.

Somewhere along the line, Tom McMurray (or his wife) decided to move to California, where he wound up working for Governor Ronald Reagan. Had Tom not died young (heart attack), he probably would have wound up with a good job in Washington, DC, when Reagan finally made it to the White House in 1980.

Spring Valley was a divided community—Italians and something else, I don't remember what. Anyway, they fought about everything. I made the mistake of hiring a good-looking young woman (her previous experience was as clerk at a bowling alley) as my resident editor. One day, a local bank told us they'd already paid their bill which we were trying to collect again—and we found out that she'd cashed the check and kept the money. I probably should have put her in jail, but I just fired her. And hired the wife of our sports reporter, a high school teacher, sight unseen. In fact, I don't think I ever met her. The last couple years I owned the paper I seldom went to Spring Valley. Finally, I sold it two young men from St. Louis.

The Canton Community Sentinel. Finally I decided to take the battle for local supremacy rights to the home ground of the *Canton Daily Ledger*—and started a new weekly newspaper in Canton. About the same time, I purchased the only commercial printing plant in Canton, the Babcock Job Printery. I ran it as a separate operation for awhile, but finally moved it to the building in Lewistown where I had first started. I'd had to buy that building because, on the attorney's advice, I'd broken the lease when I moved. The owners threatened to sue, so he figured it would be cheaper to buy it than to fight the lawsuit. It was in that same time period that I became a candidate for delegate to the Illinois Constitutional Convention, but didn't make the final cut. Those elected were mostly lawyers and political activists.

In Canton, a stroke of luck, and a minor stroke of genius. The luck was that through an unexpected election outcome, a write-in candidate for mayor won out over the incumbent, who was supported by the Canton daily paper. We didn't support the upstart candidate all that much, but he thought we had—and wanted to give us the city's legal printing.

The paper I'd started at Hennepin, next to Spring Valley, was going nowhere fast. I read up on the Illinois statutes concerning legal publications, and found that though a new paper had to have been published for six months (which my *Sentinel* had not yet been), if the new paper was merged with another one that was a legal newspaper, then the new paper would be legal also. So, of course, I just merged the Hennepin paper with the Canton paper—*voila!* The *Sentinel* was legal—and I gained a few thousand dollars worth of city publications! About this time, we began publishing one combined newspaper section that appeared in all three of our papers in that county: *Fulton County LIFE*. We had done the same thing with the Washington and Morton publications to serve advertisers who needed coverage in both of these two Peoria suburban bedroom communities.

I expanded my real estate holdings by buying a downtown building in Canton to house *The Sentinel* offices, and hired two women to run it. Neither had any newspaper experience, but then hardly any of the then 40 or more people who were working for me had any previous training either. I tried to hire good people, and found them eager and able to learn on the job.

And when I had a chance to buy a building to house *The Courier*, I convinced my manager there, Roger Hagel, to buy it, and rent it to me. It was a no-brainer for him, as the rent equaled his payments. I was never able to pay him what he was really worth, and in this way I could even the score. When I left the newspaper business, I sold the paper to him on what I considered to be favorable terms.

And Some Losers. Two stand out. One was a newspaper started in Peoria by a young African American and produced and printed in my plant. It went well for a few weeks, and then his check bounced. I went looking for him. Turned out he'd been arrested for drunk driving or something, got out on bail, and left the city. I looked through the window of his office and saw stacks and stacks of newspapers. He'd never circulated any of them, except to advertisers. And I imagine most of his advertising was obtained by playing the race card.

The other one was at Quincy, Illinois. This guy had been a legislative assistant, or campaign manager for a congressional candidate. Anyway, when his man lost the election, the campaign manager came up with the money to start a conservative weekly in Quincy. His journalism knowledge was nonexistent and most weeks he'd show up with boxes of stuff that we'd have to work half the night to transform into a newspaper. (Marvin, the original guy at Morton, would pull the same trick. I remember one night actually falling asleep while typing copy at the keyboard!)

Anyway, after a few months the Quincy guy's check also bounced. And he wouldn't talk to me on the phone. So I drove my station wagon to Quincy, found his office, and walked in and loaded up everything that appeared to have some value. Turned out the best of the equipment wasn't paid for, so I had to assume the balance of the payments. But it made me feel better.

Otherwise, we'd occasionally get some web press work from Peoria through Roger Hagel. And I printed the local college weekly paper, and a non-official college paper at Macomb. Plus the Canton high school paper, which also was weekly, I think.

Cutting Edge Stuff. What we didn't have in equipment or finances (and we were always short of both) I had to make up for with innovation. When we switched, early-on, to phototypesetting, we had two keyboards which punched paper tape that was in turn fed into the phototypesetter. So I had to come up with a system so that the women typists would be working on the right copy at the right time.

Geezer Glances

Putting numbers on an experience impairs pleasure. Picasso once said, "If you love a woman, you don't measure her legs."

The poet Robert Browning said, "Take away love and our earth is a tomb." One hundred years or so later, Albert Camus formulated an equally indisputable truth: "Without work all life goes rotten. But when work is soulless, life stifles and dies."

But, as Santayana pointed out, "Life is not a spectacle or a feast; it is a predicament." The "predicament" has to do not only with fulfilling ourselves in work and in love, but with resolving the inevitable conflict between the two. Work affirms and defines the self; loving dissolves and obliterates it. Work is structure and order; love is freedom. Work is oriented to the future, to goals; love demands the present. Work is domination and mastery; love is receptivity and submission. Work is mind; love is feeling.

As Kierkegaard said, "Life can only be understood backward, but it must be lived forward." But by understanding this predicament, inspecting its sources, and gaining insight into the inner dynamics of work and love, we may be better equipped to approach our own crucial balances.

I used wire baskets hung on the wall, in the routine order to match the press time/day involved. But then I had to also allow for work involving the ads which, of course, often had to be completed ahead of the time when the news matter would be needed. So we made paper folders of different colors for the ad copy and commercial printing work.

And I went one step further. A red folder meant do this next, stopping work on whatever you're doing, and hand-carry it to the next work station. A yellow (or maybe green) folder meant do as soon as you finish what you're working on. Simple, as are most good systems, and it worked. I have always felt that to have a "fool-proof" system, it is important not to have a fool devising the system.

Most newspapers in those days were 8-and sometimes 9-columns wide, and 5 or 6 columns on tabloid-size pages. Each column was just short of two inches wide. But the phototypesetting paper came in 3-inch widths or wider, which meant we wasted a bit more than a third of it. Plus, it takes a lot of time to paste-up a page when there are so many columns.

So I came up with a great idea. We'd have 9 columns of advertising (which meant more dollars' worth of advertising to a page), but only six columns of news—the news columns being nearly 3 inches wide. In practice, it worked out that for every two columns of news, there were three columns of ads. So the only trick was to lay out the ads so that they would be even horizontally at the top in 3, 6 or 9 column groups. Not a problem really. For tabloids, the same width of columns worked out to four news columns over six ad columns. It was an advantage in every respect. It's faster to typeset the longer line of news copy, because fewer lines had to be hyphenated. And page make-up went at least a third faster than the old way. Plus, we didn't have to waste a third of the expensive phototypesetting paper anymore. As far as I know, I was the first to do this. And I should have patented the idea! Now, it is in common use.

When we first bought the Washington paper, we installed teletype machines for quick communication between offices. But it was never really practical. So we had them taken out and tried an early version of the fax machine. This one worked by scanning copy fastened to a cylinder—took about 5 minutes for an 8 1/2 x 11 sheet. (It saved time/money if the copy was single spaced!) We also utilized the C.B. radio system for local communication.

Finally, we settled on an outgoing 800-number phone line. The other offices were called at set times. Or, if they needed to talk to me at other times, they'd call for me person to person, and be told I wasn't in. And then we'd call them back on the 800 line.

One month, I noticed that the 800 number line charges had greatly increased. I challenged the phone company, and they discovered that the timing device was malfunctioning. "Great," I said. "This'll make a good story to tell in my newspaper." Oh, don't do that, they said. Just tell us how much you think you've been overcharged, and we'll credit your account. The power of the press!

In the end—and all good things must end, you know—I signed most of it over to my ex-wife after selling the Spring Valley paper to two young men, and the Washington paper to its manager, Roger Hagel. I started my new life with less than a thousand dollars and a firm conviction that, having succeeded in something once, the second time should be easier. It wasn't, but it did turn out to be possible. And making the change probably saved me from an early death from stress-related causes.

THE THREE BIGGEST ADVERTISING LIES:
1) Tastes as good as homemade.
2) Last month my bust gained three inches.
3) Fast, effective relief from the pain of hemorrhoids.
—Howard Smith, Village Voice columnist, in his book, *The Three Biggest Lies*, Bantam

Show Biz Was My Life!

Several of my more "interesting" careers involved show business, more or less.

For a couple of years, when I first moved to Nashville, I served as "personal manager" for a country music recording star, then became a music journalist for a fledgling (and eventually a failing) biweekly magazine for new-generation fans of country music. Next came a position as vice president for public relations of another fledgling (and failing) enterprise—an independent record label. And that led to ownership and eventual sale of a small phonograph record manufacturing plant.

I didn't make any real money from any of these efforts, but enough to survive. And with a few bucks profit from sale of the plant, I finally found a position as copywriter in the advertising department of a publishing company operated by one of the major mainstream protestant religions.

Here are a few of the lessons I learned.

Music Business

If you have a quantity of "gifts" of no real intrinsic value to give away, you can actually increase their value by not giving one to everyone.

We were at "Fan Fair," an annual gathering of country music fans in Nashville that the singers attend for brief periods to sign autographs and/or to perform a song or two at showcase concerts presented by their record labels. By making use of the public address system, I'd managed to assemble a sizable crowd of my singer's fans at his booth so they could obtain the treasured signatures.

(Why do people want autographs? Simple. To prove they actually were there!)

The singer signed willingly until only a small number of fans remained, patiently waiting for their opportunity. And then he insisted he had to leave.

"Why leave now?" I asked. "In a couple more minutes, everyone could have gotten your autograph." "You don't understand," he said as we walked rapidly toward the car. "If everyone can get my autograph, then it had no value to those who felt lucky when they got one." And so, by disappointing a few, he greatly pleased the majority. Not fair!, you say? But as a friend once told me: Fair is a word used in weather forecasts!

Music Journalist

Being interviewed by a writer is a real ordeal for most stars. Mostly they are always asked the same questions: How did you get your start? (I was lucky.) Do you write your own songs? (Few do, but shy away from actually naming the writers, since most singers naturally prefer that the song be associated with them and not the writer.) Which was your favorite record? (That's like asking which of your children you love the most.)

So why do the stars agree to be interviewed? Simple. It's part of their job. The label they work for tries to convince their artists that publicity (free publicity at that) is vital to their careers, to the sale of their albums. But the celebrity is always aware that many writers come to the interview with their own agenda; some journalists seek an opportunity to "one-up" the interviewee; some want to use the access to promote their own personal celebrityhood.

Took me a while to realize that the singers I wanted to interview needed me as much as I needed them! Works that way in every business or profession. Nearly every occupation is the same—the buyer needs the seller and the seller needs the buyer. Grasp that truth and you'll succeed in any job.

Public Relations

The "bible" of the music business was Billboard magazine. Getting your company's "news" published in Billboard is the best, easiest, quickest way to spread the word among others in your segment of the business. And every business, profession, or trade has a similar publication. The music business, in fact, has several.

It is with modest pride that I announce than Billboard published every "news release" that I wrote for them. Why? First, I read every weekly issue, cover to cover—even the articles that weren't about my own segment of the music business. Thus I became knowledgeable about what its editors considered to be news.

Most important, like a songwriter, I gave each news release a "hook," an eye-catching and mind-grabbing opening that would be preferred by the editors over the customary "So-and-so company announced today that . . ." And my approach worked—every time.

Music Manufacturing

The small record-pressing plant I owned for about a year was technically bankrupt when I got involved—so we had no where to go but up. And, since it was incorporated, I had nothing to lose and everything to gain. Well, not "everything," but something, at least.

The plant was equipped to press only smaller quantities of records, so our main customers were musicians/singers who played the "lounge circuit" and wanted an album to sell to their nightly audiences. An order for 1,000 to 5,000 records was a normal quantity. About half of the retail price would be clear profit to the seller—or maybe more than half, since it's doubtful that income taxes were ever collected on these cash transactions.

Our first order of business was to survive. How could we reach our prospects? There's no directory of small-time bands or wanna-be singing stars! So I wrote and published a small pamphlet I titled "So You Want to Make a Record." It was designed to fit into a business-size envelope along with our standard price lists.

I purchased small classified ads in various publications read by most musicians and offered a free copy of the booklet, which of course touted my company's services, along with other advice on how to obtain financing, how to promote their albums, and how to deal with copyrights and so on.

The requests arrived and the orders followed in satisfactory numbers. And I then promptly—and wisely—sold the company.

Secrets of Successful Advertising

As a newspaper publisher earlier in life, my concerns about advertising were centered on how to sell more of it since over half of the cost of newspaper printing and distribution were paid for by advertising revenues. And, face it, in a relatively small universe of readers of my small-city newspapers, the actual words in the ad probably were not as important as the fact that the ad was published.

But now I faced a different situation. The religious publishing and mail-order seller of all manner of church supplies I worked for had mailing lists in the hundreds of thousands. And budgets in the millions of dollars. And so our advertising copy had to be carefully and thoughtfully crafted to obtain the maximum return of orders.

These are the essential patterns that worked:

1. Don't talk about what "we" can offer; talk about what "you" will gain from your purchase. And don't discuss the product's features; talk about its benefits. Or, as Elmer Wheeler once wrote, "sell the sizzle, not the steak."

2. Not using language that would turn people off was more important than trying to find words that would turn them on to the product or service.

3. When you find something that works—an approach that produces a profitable response—use the same approach again. And again. If it worked once, it'll work twice. And again and again.

By the way, for some reason the "rule of 3" works. For example, if you're using adjectives to describe the product's "sizzle," use three adjectives, not two, not four.

Here's another example—three rules for a successful life:

1. Never play poker with a man named "Doc."
2. Never eat at a restaurant called "Mom's Place."
3. Never fall in love with anyone who has more problems than you do.

Geezer Gems

Whatever you have received more than others in health, in talents, in ability, in success, in a pleasant childhood, in harmonious conditions of home life—all this you must not take to yourself as a matter of course. You must pay a price for it. You must render, in return, an unusually great sacrifice of your life for other life.—Dr. Albert Schweitzer:

To which I add: Perhaps, but if so, then the opposite must also apply. If your life has thus far been filled with tragedy, misfortune, mistakes, and all of the ills that might befall a human, you have a right—a duty in fact—to expect, to seek, to find ways to bring into your life the joy, happiness, and fulfillment that you desire. It is yours: take it.

Paul says in the Bible: Whatsoever things are true, whatsoever things are honest, whatsoever things are just, whatsoever things are pure, whatsoever things are lovely, whatsoever things are of good report; if there be any virtue, and if there be any praise, think on these things. (Phil. 4:8)

I think Paul meant that you should "put into your mind, into your daily life all of the 'good' things that you seek, all of the 'good' feelings you wish to experience—and you'll get 'em!"

> Work consists of whatever a body is obliged to do, and
> Play consists of whatever a body is not obliged to do.
> —Mark Twain, *The Adventures of Huckleberry Finn*

Find a Job You Love and Never Work Again!

Sometimes I believe that it is true: Our thoughts can become our reality. Certainly, your life will be filled with many happy coincidences, just as mine has been.

The story of how I happened to become a writer is a good example. As a youngster, I felt out of place in a Nebraska family during the dust storms, drouth, and economic depression of the 1930s. My father raised cattle, and farmed relatively few acres that lay in a valley surrounded by our pastures and hayfields in the grassy sandhills.

With four older brothers and, later, three younger sisters, I was somehow caught in the middle, and so I found solace in reading. So it is no surprise that this led me to aspire to a career as a writer—and I sold my first "article" to the Nebraska Farmer magazine when I was still in elementary school. It earned me only a dollar—it was a brief "helpful farm hint" that I adapted from something I'd read in another magazine. And I'd like to say I still have that one-dollar check—but of course I don't. And, of course I didn't realize then that it was wrong to "steal" another writer's idea. But I did rewrite it, in my own words.

After a couple of years of service in the U.S. Coast Guard during World War II's waning months, I decided to use my G.I. Bill benefits and attend the school of journalism at the University of Colorado. But it was not to be. Instead, while spending my first summer as a civilian with my family, giving their home a badly needed coat of paint, I was stricken with appendicitis—and the resulting surgery and hospital stay wiped out my savings. Today's VA hospitals were not yet built.

What now? In the Omaha newspaper I saw an advertisement for a railroad telegraphers school. I'd been trained as a radio operator, knew Morse code, and decided to use my educational benefits to qualify for what was then a well-paying job.

Thus one sunny August day I boarded the train for Omaha. I happened to sit by a red-haired woman who turned out to be a hometown native married to an Omahan—and he happened to be an instructor at the very school where I planned to enroll. She tipped me off to the fact that railroads were switching to teletype and, she quoted her husband, jobs for the telegraphers he trained would soon be few and far between. When I told her my of my writing ambitions, she suggested I attend Omaha Tech (where her daughter was a student) because it had a complete printing and journalism sequence.

She invited me to her home the next day to meet her daughter who, she said, would be happy to take me to the school and show me around. When I saw her daughter—also a redhead—I decided on the spot to enroll in Omaha Tech. As it turned out, I did date Louise several times. But then I fell in love with Beverly, a dark-haired beauty who was majoring in art.

Tech was great, as most of the students there were only about a year younger than I was, yet none had been in the service—so I was a Big Man on Campus, so to speak. I soon was promoted to managing editor of the school paper and began learning how to write, and how to edit the writings of others.

I got a monthly check from the VA—not much—so I found a job at the Hilltop House, one of Omaha's top restaurants of the day.

(It was the place where movie stars ate when they came to town.) I started as a bus boy, but lost interest when another bus boy dumped a tray of dishes and the cost was deducted from his pay. So I transferred to dishwashing, and later moved up to salad boy (fixing the fixings). I got paid a few bucks and I ate dinner there free each night.

In all, I was only in Omaha for one semester. But I am getting ahead of myself. After a while the restaurant job began interfering with my social life, so I looked for Saturday daytime employment. I found it at a little clothing and jewelry store in downtown Omaha.

The owner gave me careful training. Mostly I operated as a stock boy and janitor. But when the boss was busy, I could take care of customers up to the point of ringing up the sale. No one got into the cash register except the boss! Also, he warned me to stay away from him whenever he had a "big customer."

"Don't even let him catch your eye," he said. "It might be just enough to cause me to lose the sale."

White shirts were said to be in short supply then (a shortage caused by the war) so he had only one or two in each size on display. But in the backroom were boxes and boxes of white shirts. "As long as people think they're scarce, they'll keep buying them," he explained.

Then near the end of the semester, one of my teachers introduced me to a friend of hers, Al Horlings, who had recently bought a newspaper in Manhattan, Kansas. He interviewed me by telephone and hired me as a reporter. I would start work in January on the GI Bill's On-the-Job Training Program. The idea was for the government to supplement your earnings on a declining basis over a two-year-period with the employer making matching salary increases so you would earn as much from the beginning as you otherwise would be paid after two years. Al explained that he had taught journalism at Kansas State College and that I could enroll for some courses if I wished. Sounded like a good deal to me, so I accepted.

So, barely 19 years old, I became a "professional writer," a journalist with a paycheck to prove it. Ten years later, I bought my own newspaper, and added seven more before starting a new career as a magazine writer, then another as an advertising copywriter.

College? Regretfully, I just never found time for it. Within a couple of years on my first job, I was that newspaper's managing editor with authority to hire and fire college graduates. Oh, I have enrolled in some college courses over the years, but mostly for personal growth reasons. But I'm not recommending this kind of career short cut today.

"Find a job you love," I was once advised, "and you'll never work another day in your life." My life is a testament to that counsel. And it all began the day I struck up a conversation with a redheaded woman on a train!

Geezer Glimpses

A creator needs only one enthusiast to justify him.—Man Ray

The greatest invention of the 19th century was the invention of the method of invention.—Alfred North Whitehead

I don't think necessity is the mother of invention. Invention, in my opinion, arises directly from idleness, possibly also from laziness. To save oneself trouble.—Agatha Christie

Never doubt that a small group of thoughtful, committed citizens can change the world; indeed, it is the only thing that ever has.—Margaret Mead

> Power tends to corrupt; absolute power corrupts absolutely.
> —Lord Acton in a letter to Bishop Creighton

A Lesson in Power vs. Control

A lot of things—both good and bad—happened during my years working for a newspaper in Phillipsburg, Kansas.

After a few years as a reporter and ad salesman, I became editor of the paper when the owner went to Topeka as executive secretary to the governor. My tower of power was shared to a degree with the head printer, whose name was Merlyn—a local man who had never worked anywhere else. He resisted my authority whenever possible, and could make life difficult for me on such matters as getting things printed by the date I'd promised them, and so forth.

Once a year, second class mail publications like the one I worked for have to file with the post office and also print in the paper or magazine a document called "Statement of Ownership, Management and Circulation." As editor, I of course completed the form, signed it, and filed it with the postmaster. I also turned in a duplicate copy to be typeset and published.

But when the next issue of the paper was printed, I saw that Merlyn had taken my name out as "editor" and replaced it with the absentee owner's name instead. I immediately told him that he shouldn't have done that, since the published version had to agree with the version I'd filed, and there was no way the owner could get home to sign it, etc., etc. His reply was to the effect that he worked for the owner and not for me; ergo the owner must be the editor because everybody knew that the editor was the man who owned the newspaper and I sure didn't own it!

I explained the mixup to the postmaster's satisfaction and the next time I saw the owner, I told him that either Merlyn went or I would. All right, he said, you want to get rid of him, you fire him. OK, I said. Now who will we get to take his place? That's your problem, not mine, he replied. I saw immediately that he'd trumped my ace. Where in Western Kansas, where towns—not to mention trained printers—were few and far between, would I find another person who could take charge of our printing department?

So Merlyn stayed, and so did I. For a while. And very aware of the lesson I had learned about the difference between "power" and "control." Later, I also discovered that the best way to stay in power is to not be goaded into trying to prove that you have power.

> It is often easier to fight for principles then to live up to them.
> —Adlai Stevenson, in a New York City speech

You Have to Take a Stand Sometimes

In nearly every respect that I'm aware of, I've always prided myself in being a law-abiding citizen. I even halt at stop signs—including those on country roads where no other traffic is in sight! And, as a journalist for much of my life, I've often worked in close association with law enforcement personnel and, in most cases, found them personally worthy of respect.

But there are always exceptions to every rule, it seems. And, when confronted by an exception, one must make an often-difficult decision as to just who actually represents the law—you or the person wearing the badge.

As a young reporter and a veteran, I was once elected as an officer of the local post of a veteran's organization. In that capacity and during the Korean Conflict, a neatly dressed man, wearing a hat, approached me on the sidewalk outside of the newspaper office. He confirmed my identity, then showed me his FBI badge, and invited me to join him in the front seat of his rather ordinary-looking sedan—the one with the strange little radio antenna protruding from the luggage compartment.

Turned out he had checked my background and proposed

that I serve as an undercover information source in my community. Why? The reason he cited was the presence there of a large oil refinery that, he indicated, possibly could be the target of Communist skulduggery. Flattered, I accepted.

The first few months, as instructed, I would call an unlisted telephone number and report any suspicious persons or activity or report that there was nothing to report—the latter always being the case.

Then the agent contacted me again with suspicions about a local attorney, an active Democrat and a fairly liberal-minded man whose wife was the local postmistress by virtue, so I understood, of her past service to the Democratic Party, the postal service having not yet been removed from politics. Though the community usually voted Republican, the attorney and the postmistress were well regarded by everyone that I knew, and their son was an after-school employee of the newspaper where I worked.

I decided I did not want to continue to take part in what seemed to me to be a politically-inspired witch hunt, and stopped making my monthly "no reports" calls. After a time, the county sheriff told me that the FBI was inquiring about me, and I told him that I had no connection with them.

I heard nothing further from the sheriff or the agent. But to this day I wonder what is in my "file" at FBI headquarters.

A few years later, I was publishing a newspaper in Illinois. One day as some printing equipment was being moved into my printing plant, one of the workmen moved my car from its normal parking place in front of the loading dock and parked it in a no-parking zone for the few minutes needed to unload the truck.

But in those few minutes, one of the local city policemen came by on his rounds of checking parking meters, saw the car, and wrote a ticket. As of course he should have done.

What he should not have done, however, was stop me on the street the next day to verbally "dress me down," warning me that he "had been keeping an eye on you since you came to this town," and other such nonsense. I didn't know it at the time, but later learned he was a good friend of the publisher of a competing local weekly newspaper, who in turn, was a friend and supporter of the mayor—a coal mining superintendent who patterned his political conduct after that of the infamous mayor of Chicago, William J. Daley.

Immediately after this confrontation, I returned to my office and wrote an editorial about the events involving my car and the policeman. I noted that although I didn't park the car there myself, it was my car and it was in a no parking zone, and so I would not contest the fine. But I would contest the right of the city policeman to verbally abuse me as he had done.

The response overwhelmed me. Shortly after that day's edition of my newspaper hit the streets, every available copy had been sold. People stopped by my home all evening, many bearing gifts of food, and all telling stories of how this same policeman had berated them for such minor offenses as failing to put enough change in their parking meter. One housewife said he'd even drawn his gun when she had objected to his abusive language.

Turned out the policeman's only previous training had been as a state prison guard. By the end of the week, he had resigned and left town. The local judge offered to waive my fine, but I insisted on paying it. My car was ticketed in a no parking zone, after all. So I had broken the law. But, unlike the former policeman, at least I had not abused it!

Geezer Gleanings

"The clever and beautiful need not be proud, since they did nothing to earn their advantages.

"The ignorant and ugly need not be ashamed, since they did nothing to deserve their fate.

"The hateful need not be blamed, since they did not make themselves hateful, nor need the loving be praised, for the same reason."

—Eric Berne, M.D., in *A Layman's Guide to Psychiatry & Psychoanalysis.*

I am only one,
But still I am one.
I cannot do everything,
But still I can do something;
And because I cannot do everything
I will not refuse to do the something that I can do.
—Edward Everett Hale, for the Lend-a-Hand Society

What men call gallantry, and gods adultery,
Is much more common where the climate's sultry.
—Byron: *Don Juan*

> The propensity to truck, barter, and exchange . . . is common to all men, and to be found in no other race of animals.
> —Adam Smith: *The Wealth of Nations*

First, Make a Good Impression

When you move to a new rural community or even to a different suburban location, always remember that the first impression that you give your neighbors is likely how they always will think of you.

When I moved to the Cumberland Plateau in Tennessee, I brought with me an old—really old—full-size pick-up truck. One day not long before I moved, I was driving it down the 6-lane interstate highway in city traffic when I lost the clutch linkage. I was never enough of a mechanic to fix such things, so with the help of a friend, we towed it to a combination auto junkyard and mechanic's garage at the next exit. The proprietor had enough other old pick-ups on the lot to supply any needed parts, and in due time, the truck was ready to use.

But there was a problem. Every time I stopped for a traffic light, the motor would die. I looked under the hood and discovered that the carburetor controls were strung this way and that—with screen door springs! I could never figure out how to make a better repair, so I managed to tighten one spring a little and stretch the opposite one a little—and it worked!

Then, one day, it died on my farm's driveway, and nothing I

tried would revive it. I was commuting over 100 miles to work each day and, with a lot of other things needing my attention at home, I just let the truck sit for a while.

When a young man from the neighborhood drove in one day and asked if the truck was for sale, I quickly said, yes, it was. Doesn't run, I said, but probably needs a different carburetor—and I showed him the screen door spring arrangement.

He sort of whistled between his teeth at the sight of it and then asked, "What are you asking for it?" $500, I said. He whistled again, then said, "How much you figure you gotta have for it?" I held firm at $500, and told him where I thought he might be able to pick up a good used carburetor. So we shook hands, and he said he'd be back to "get 'er runnin'."

And he did. Took him a couple of evenings and a bit of fooling with wrenches and screwdrivers, and then he fired it up, wheeled it around in front of my house, revved it up good, and turned it off. His buddy remained at the wheel of the car they came in.

"Here's the thing," he said. "I've only got $400, but I thought since you just moved out here, there might be something I've got that you'd take in trade for the other $100."

I gave his proposal the due consideration it required, and then said, "Well, yes. There's a bunch of groundhogs digging holes down there around the foundation of the barn. I guess I could use a good .22 rifle so I could get rid of them."

"Great," he said. "I've got just what you need. I'll bring it by tomorrow evening."

He did, and it was a well-used, but well-maintained bolt action .22—the kind that looked as if it probably didn't cost more than $100 when it was brand new—however long ago that may have been.

So, we made the deal, and he went back to the truck, started it up, then leaned out the window and said:

"I gotta be honest with you," he said. "That rifle probably isn't worth the $100."

"That's okay," I said. "I probably would have sold you the pick-up for $250."

We both laughed, and he waved and drove off. Me, I felt that my reputation as a person who couldn't be easily snookered on a trade was now a well-established fact in that neighborhood. And it was.

A few years later, when I was selling off most of my personal property prior to moving again, a man came to buy my automatic washer and dryer. When he saw the rifle leaning in the corner next to the front door, next to a baseball bat I kept handy for the same reason, he asked if the gun was for sale. No, I said, I was planning on giving that to my grandson. And of course I had to tell the guy my story of how I got the rifle.

"I'll give you a hundred for it," he said, and peeled off a pair of 50s. I took it. What else could I do?

But, you know, ever since then I've been wondering what that rifle REALLY was worth!

Geezer Giggles

CARTOON CAPTIONS

Two women talking while man with a chicken head and beak stands nearby. "I don't know what's come over him lately; he's gotten such a fowl mouth!"

Cat in a hospital bed says to doctor: "You mean to say that "Nine Lives" is just a brand of cat food?"

Disk jockey is saying: "I know this is not an FM radio station, but then I never wanted to be just another stereo type."

Geezer Grist

There is no better measure of a person than what he does when he is absolutely free to choose.—Wilma Askinas

We act as though comfort and luxury were the chief requirements of life, when all that we need to make us really happy is something to be enthusiastic about.—Charles Kingsley

The creature goes to heaven very baffled.
My God, what was all that about? it asks.
God says: Well, you were a wolf.
I see, says the wolf.

—*Esquire* November 1996, from *Two Gone Over*, short story by Barry Hannah, from his collection, *High Lonesome*.

People who think they know it all are especially annoying to those of us who do.—Anon.

> He who steals my purse steals trash;
> 'tis something, nothing;
> But he that filches from me my good name
> Robs me of that which not enriches him,
> 'Twas mine, 'tis his, and has been slave to thousands,
> And makes me poor indeed.
> —Shakespeare, *Othello, Act III*

Sow's Ears and Silk Purses

It was early winter or late spring when I boarded a bus in my hometown in Central Illinois, bound for Nashville, Tennessee. In truth, I had the money to fly to Nashville and a big car that I could have used to drive there. But I had this idea: I wanted to write a screenplay for a made-for-TV movie about a would-be songwriter who goes to Nashville, and . . .

Well, you get the idea. I wanted to experience my subject matter before I tried to get inside of someone else's skin. As part of my preparation, I had written a dozen original songs that I'd put on reel-to-reel tape, using one of those chord organs, complete with automatic rhythm accompaniment. The idea was to take those songs to various music publishers in the Music City, and experience the rejection that every "wannabe" songwriter faces.

The first leg of the trip went smoothly. Hardly anyone else was on the bus on the first leg to St. Louis, where I'd change buses for the final run to Nashville with one more bus change in

Jackson, Tennessee. I'd taken a seat near the front of the bus—if I'm not the driver then at least I want to see where I'm going—and I passed the time chatting with the driver about his experiences behind the wheel of this people mover.

As in many large cities, the St. Louis bus depot was deep in the heart of the "bad" part of town. At the time I wondered which came first—the bus depot or the poverty. Later, I saw first hand that when a bus depot relocated, it immediately attracts a congregation of unemployed hustlers of one kind and another.

But I didn't know that then. And so I didn't give it a second thought when I emerged from a stall in the men's room and found a group of young men apparently had followed me in, and were lounging around, passing a bottle of wine among them.

As I washed my hands, one of them approached, grabbed my left wrist, and examined my wristwatch—a Timex, as I remember.

"Nice watch," he said.

"Not really," I said, and jerked my arm away. At which point he demanded that I hand over the watch and my billfold. On reflex, I turned to face him and brought up my knee sharply to impact his body at a point sure to cause him pain.

Unfortunately, I'd ignored the rest of the group, and one of them struck me on the left side of my face with the wine bottle. I went down, amazed at the fireworks display that was at play in front of my eyes. When I struggled back to my feet, the watch, billfold, the young men, and a large measure of my dignity had disappeared. I bathed my face in cold water and became aware of the pain.

Just outside of the restroom door a uniformed security guard was standing. "Did you see four or five young guys come out of here?" I asked. No, he hadn't. But when I told him what happened to me, he did offer to call the police and suggested that he also summon an ambulance to take me to a hospital for treatment. I shrugged off his suggestions and, remembering that I had tucked a couple of hundred dollars and a credit card in my luggage, I sought out the baggage room.

The attendant asked for my baggage claim, but it was with my ticket, and it was gone. ID? No billfold.

"But that's my suitcase right there," I said, pointing.

"How do I know it's yours?" he asked. Open it up, I said, and there'll be a red coffeepot in there (I always travel with my own coffeemaker—got to have my caffeine first thing in the morning).

Of course the red coffeepot was there, and I found my money, bought another ticket, and rechecked the suitcase. By this time, my cheek was throbbing. I didn't even think of buying some aspirin. Instead, I asked the restaurant waitress for some ice. Apparently it was in short supply for she would give me only a small plastic cup of the cold stuff. For 50 cents.

I wrapped the ice in my handkerchief and held it against my cheek. The ice was gone before the bus cleared the city limits. Thereafter I would press my cheek against the window, which, it now being well after dark, was cool, if not cold.

The bus depot in Jackson was a one-room affair without so much as a soft drink machine. I had a one-hour layover, but then it was announced that the driver had overslept and the hour stretched into three hours. And so it was mid-morning before we finally pulled into Nashville.

The Music City's bus depot in those days was just up the street from the famed Ryman Auditorium, historic mother church of country music. Nashville's Lower Broadway district was then crowded with honkytonks and pawnshops plus, strangely, several furniture stores scattered among them. Two low-rent hotels stood just up the hill, and I took a room in the nearest one and slept for a day or two.

I had a trio of cousins who were on a record label in Nashville. So, with my face returned more or less to its original contours, I decided to walk to Music Row, stop at my relatives' studio, and then start my rounds of music publishers to experience the rejection I anticipated. On the way, I passed the offices of the two daily newspapers and—on the spur of the moment—decided to stop and tell my story about the mugging to a columnist for the afternoon paper.

I'd read the late Red O'Donnell's column in the *Nashville Banner* while I was laid up at the hotel, and being a newspaperman myself, realized that my experience was a "natural." Newspapers love those "man bites dog" stories. In this case, the story was about a writer seeking background information on a subject he intended to write about—and who got more experience than he wanted.

I was right. Red was in, listened to my tale, and said he probably could use it. I left his office, feeling something like I suppose a guy does just after he's been interviewed on TV at the scene of a tornado that just blew his house away.

"Well, we was just sittin' down at the table fer supper, and we heard this noise like a train, and next thing we knew, all hell broke loose."

At my cousins' office, I learned that my family had been calling, desperate for news of me. Someone had found my billfold—money gone but credit cards, etc., still intact—in a trashcan near the St. Louis bus depot. Unable to reach me, the family expected the worst, so I called home immediately.

Then I told my cousins of my plans, but didn't offer to play my demo tape for them, nor did they ask to hear it. They did assure me that I'd have no trouble experiencing rejection.

So off I went, up and down 16th, 17th, and 18th Avenues on "Music Row." Those streets are lined by a mixed bag of big buildings and old houses converted into offices, most of them housing enterprises connected in one way or another with music. I think I probably was trying to select one with an eye to its eventual appearance in the movie, because the first music publisher I visited was housed in a log cabin-looking house.

In those days, it wasn't cool to submit songs on a cassette, which is now the preferred medium. And on my reel-to-reel tape,

I had about a dozen songs. Later I learned that one should submit only two or three cuts. But the woman who played my tape didn't seem to mind, and listened all the way through, making a comment now and then when she heard a line she considered trite, and outright rejecting my personal favorite.

"Your song with the line, 'All I ever wanted was to hear you sing my song,' is too inside for the general public," she said. I didn't explain that the line was meant to be metaphorical, because at that moment, she added: "Okay, we'll take the first cut, the third one, and the one about the old man in the restaurant."

As she made tape copies of the three songs and prepared the copyright documents, my heart was racing, and my mind too. Who wants rejection when he can have acceptance? Who wants to write a screenplay when he's told that he's a songwriter? Not me!

It would be the perfect ending if I could tell you that all three songs were recorded, and that one of them reached the top 10.

But it didn't happen. What did happen was that when Red O'Donnell's column was published that afternoon, I became the "flavor of the day" on Music Row. Everyone I met the next day or two seemed to have read the story of my St. Louis adventure. One bass player in the band of one of my favorite singers wanted to hear my songs, and decided to go into the studio that night and record one of them. He made all the arrangements, and then left the studio to, as he put it, "go score some dope." I asked the engineer if I could use the phone to call a cab. "Good idea," he said.

Back home a few days later, a letter from the president of the bus company was waiting for me. It seemed that O'Donnell also used the story about me in his syndicated column, and the executive wanted to apologize. I might have taken his apology more seriously if he had enclosed a refund for the stolen ticket. But he didn't.

The screenplay forgotten, I wrote an account of the experience in my own newspaper column, and concluded that, on balance, I would rather be the victim of a mugging than be the persons doing the mugging. My few losses were covered by insurance. But those young toughs may still be struggling to regain their self-respect.

Me? I have my self-respect! Why not? After all, I've had three songs accepted by a publisher . . . and maybe, just maybe, one day I'll write one that actually will be recorded!

Geezer Gripes

April 22 is the anniversary of Earth Day, begun in 1970 to focus more public attention on environmental concerns. How easily those words roll off the tongue or keyboard—but how difficult it seems to get people actually totally committed to the task of preserving our planet.

Eight years before Earth Day started, Rachel Carson wrote *Silent Spring*, the classic argument against continuing to unbalance nature by overuse of pesticides and herbicides. Much has been learned—but few seem to have learned it—in those intervening three decades.

The Amish have a saying, I am told:
We didn't inherit the land from our fathers,
We are borrowing it from our children.

Giving it to our children in better condition than we found it would still make it a low-interest loan.

LIVE WELL

> Ye are better than all the ballads
> That were ever sung or said;
> For ye are the living poems,
> And all the rest are dead.

Henry Wadsworth Longfellow: *Children*

Geezer Gifts

"It's probably foolish not to believe in God. What's the point in not believing? What have you got to lose?"—Don Imus, radio talk show legend, quoted by Jeffrey Zazlow in *USA Weekend* July 7-9, 1995

"It is inconceivable that God would break the laws of nature he created in order to persuade mankind through miraculous acts. It is far more logical to believe Jesus and his disciples performed miracles in the early days of Christianity as the result of natural phenomena known by God but entirely unknown to us."—Leon Hurlburt Lehman, Belo Horizonte, Brazil, in letter published in *Time*, May 8, 1995

"It is not disbelief that is dangerous to our society; it is belief."—George Bernard Show: Preface to *Androcles and the Lion*

> Oh, what a tangled web we weave
> When first we practice to deceive!
> —Sir Walter Scott, *Marmion VI*

More Work Than Working

Boot camp was not designed to make life easy for would-be sailors.

Straggling down the street between barracks when we arrived, we were greeted by shouts of "you'll be sorry." And we soon were.

Physicals, a weekly round of shots, hour after hour of drilling, cleaning the barracks, keeping our beds made and our gear stored properly, marching in the Saturday morning parade. daily inspections: all were designed to weed out the weaklings and train the survivors to act as a unit, immediately obeying every order without taking time to think about it.

You were frequently reminded that the government was not paying you to think, because the officers and non-coms were there to fulfill that role. Your only job was to obey. Instantly. Without question.

Because I was tall, I marched at the head of one line of men when in formation. So I had one advantage—I led my column of men into the mess hall at mealtime. A small satisfaction, but it was the only one I had!

After a few weeks, our drill instructor announced one Friday morning that the following week we would receive swimming instruction, including practice in jumping off of a ship into the ocean. Non-swimmers, he said, should proceed to the pool facility immediately so they could receive an additional day of training.

Well, I could swim—a little. Enough. But, I thought (forgetting we'd been told that we weren't being paid to think) if I fell out with the non-swimmers, maybe we wouldn't have to jump off the tower that simulated a ship. Or at least, not as often as would be expected of the good swimmers.

Within an hour, the swimming instructors had taken us through the paces, designed to discover those who were totally helpless in water. I wasn't, of course, and was rather proud to be quickly moved to the "skilled" group.

But then, the "skilled" group was moved immediately to the tower. And each of us was required to jump. In my mind, the tower must have been six stories tall—but probably it was only half that high. Anyway, I had no trouble making the leap. One man froze, but was finally coaxed to the edge, "just to see that it isn't that far down." But when he looked over the edge, the instructor pushed him and down he fell, arms and legs thrashing.

And so the payoff for me was that because I tried to out-think my drill officer, I had to jump off the tower six times. Those who admitted they knew how to swim had to jump only five times!

Honesty IS the best policy!

> Avarice is generally the last passion of those lives of which the first part has been squandered in pleasure, and the second devoted to ambition.
> —Samuel Johnson: *The Rambler*

Greed Is Its Own Reward

I wanted for many years to experience life in France. Then I met a French family while vacationing in Tunisia and, at their invitation, visited them again a few months later at their home in a small rural village about an hour from Paris. We came to an agreement that provided I could have separate quarters (bedroom, living room, and bathroom) but would eat with the family.

It is ideal for a semi-retired and divorced freelance writer. A place to write, free of unwanted distractions but also free of the need to prepare my meals, grocery shop, and deal with monthly utility bills, etc. Plus, space in the garage for my own car, and the opportunity to learn to speak French and experience European cultures without going cold turkey, so to speak.

But I'd lived on my own little tree and grass retirement farm near Nashville, Tennessee, for about eight years. And I had a barn, garage, and a five-room house well-filled with books, furniture, appliances, and just plain stuff. Stuff that I used occasionally and stuff that I'd acquired on the off chance that I might need or want it someday.

First, I needed to sell my land and buildings. Calling on my experience as an advertising copywriter, I dashed off a good-sized classified display ad. But how much should I ask for the selling price? A real estate broker had once told me that he could get $100,000 for it. I estimated $1,000 an acre with about $40,000 to $50,000 for the buildings. That indeed added up to about $100,000 and represented what I considered a fair profit over what I'd paid—and it sold in three days!

Unfortunately, the "buyer" didn't anticipate the difficulty of obtaining a mortgage on farmland—lenders limit you to five acres and a house. But, no problem. I got to keep the earnest money, and re-advertised the property, but this time for almost exactly twice the amount I'd paid for it 10 years earlier. Again, it sold in three days—this time to a family with sufficient equity in their city house so that they could borrow the money even before selling their present home.

Even so, my friends and relatives exclaimed that I'd sold too cheap. In truth, subdividing the farm into small tracts would have brought me a larger return. My soul would have suffered remorse from breaking up that beautiful valley into suburban type lots. And, I was satisfied. Greed, I told myself, is always rewarded by a matching loss on some other transaction.

With several weeks remaining before my departure, I rented storage space for my books and other articles that I wanted to keep for my eventual return to my native land, or that weren't practical to ship by air because of the expense. If or when I decided to remain an expatriate, I would have those belongings forwarded by ship—takes longer but costs less than air freight.

That done, I began a second advertising program to sell the furniture. Many items, such as clothing no longer in style or that didn't fit plus other things of small value, I donated to a church group serving the poor, and to the Salvation Army store.

I decided on selling prices for larger items, and in truth, my pricing must have been on the low side of value as most things sold quickly via an ad in the local weekly newspaper.

The bed, for example, went the second day. But the buyer wasn't interested in a bedroom dresser with mirror and matching bedside stand, so I cut the price on these remaining pieces to $120.

There was only one offer—$75 for both items. Oh, no, I said, I think they are worth more than that—at least $100. But no other prospective buyers showed interest.

I had a back-up plan. I had considered holding a public auction of all of my personal property, but when two auctioneers told me that I didn't have enough to make it worth their while, I made arrangements with one of them to auction my unsold stuff at a larger household sale he was holding in nearby Murfreesboro, a fast-growing small city.

So early on a Saturday morning, following a rainy Friday, I loaded the bedroom furniture into my mini-pickup truck, along with other things I'd had no offers for: a small air conditioner, kitchen counter appliances, a never-used electric baseboard heater, fire extinguishers, and a room-size rag rug.

I didn't stay for the auction; I had also advertised my pickup and car, and I expected a prospect or two to come to look at them that afternoon.

A few days later, the auctioneer phoned. I had been told by people who knew that he was the most honest of his trade in the area. So I had no doubts when he told me, with some hesitation, that my items had sold for a total of $18.00!

I suppose he wondered why I laughed, but I immediately saw the irony of my situation. For the furniture—together with my many other articles—had sold in total for about half the number of dollars I would have "lost" had I accepted the $75 offer for the furniture.

Still, there was one consolation: The auctioneer did not deduct his 10% commission!

Geezer Guidelines

... [M]ental health is based on a certain degree of tension, the tension between what one has already achieved and what one still ought to accomplish, or the gap between what one is and what one should become.... What man actually needs is not a tensionless state but rather the striving and struggling for some goal worthy of him.—Dr. Victor Frankl: *Man's Search for Meaning*

I've been freed from the self that pretends to be someone, and in becoming no-one, I begin to live. It is worthwhile dying, to find out what life is.—T.S. Elliot

While aggression can be seen to underlie goal-directed, future-oriented behavior, the sexual instinct underlies an immersion in the present. Aggression fosters change . . . while sex promotes incorporation and fusion. If aggression seeks to transform an object, sex may be seen as seeking to transform the subject. Loving fosters empathy and merging . . . an immersion in their sensations without attention to ulterior goals. . . . Aggression drives us to 'do' something (or 'make' something) with those feelings. . . . The excitement of sexual loving, whether the object is a friend, a flower, a gleaming new sports car . . . is the excitement of pleasure. In contrast to the pleasure of sexual love is the feeling of satisfaction associated with the accomplishment of aggressive work. [As in the old adage] never mix business with pleasure.—From Jay B. Rohrlich, M.D.: *Work and Love*

> There is no better measure of a person than what he does when he is absolutely free to choose.
> —Wilma Askinas

It's Hard to be a Christian Soldier . . . *

My parents were Roman Catholic and I was graduated from a Catholic High School. But I was never comfortable with the faith. In fact, I've often told the story of how I was able to obtain my high school diploma at the age of 16 after only 3 1/2 years of classes.

I would be 17 in January, just after the end of the first semester of my senior year, and I wanted to enlist in the Navy. My parents said they would agree, but only if I finished high school first. So I approached the school's principal, a Dominican nun, to see if she knew a solution to my problem.

Now, I had not been exactly the type of student the good sisters cherished. Since the school was several miles from my home, my parents allowed me to live in town in rented quarters where I did my own cooking and housekeeping—a minimal amount of each, to be sure. Often a fellow student would be dispatched from school to arouse me from my late morning slumbers and escort me to class when I failed to show up at the beginning bell.

So it is possible that the head sister viewed my desire to finish my education early as a gift from God. At any rate, she found a novel solution. And possibly would have flunked a test on ethics!

I was only one semester short of one more subject needed for graduation. The solution: She changed the name of the "religion" course (which was a Catholic-required but not a state-approved subject) to "ethics" (which was approved). And off I went to boot camp, and had the good fortune to return home on leave the very weekend of my high school graduation.

Years later, married and with one child, we began to attend a local Methodist church in the town where I was working. Moving finally to the city where I'd gone into business, I also attended the Methodist church. I did consider moving my worship to another church the Sunday morning when my beagle hound somehow escaped from the back porch of my nearby home, and tracked me down so he could harmonize his howls with the singing of the choir.

What finally ended my attendance there were two events. In Sunday school class one morning, the teacher informed us that God did not create black people to live in equality with white people. I stopped attending Sunday school, though most people attended the classes but boycotted the following worship service because they did not like the pastor. He was an older man, originally from Great Britain which, as far as I could learn, was his primary fault.

A few weeks later, the "leaders" of the congregation managed to get him transferred. After two such examples of Christian love, I decided to seek spiritual comfort elsewhere. I found it in music and in my love of nature.

* * *

* The title is from a line in a song by Billy Joe Shaver that I have heard only on a Kris Kristofferson album. Written during the Vietnam War, it goes like this: "It's hard to be a Christian soldier / When you tote a gun. / And it hurts to have to watch a grown man cry."

LAUGH OFTEN

"
And if I laugh at any mortal thing,
'Tis that I may not weep.
"

Lord Byron 1788-1824

Geezer Gospel

One ought, every day at least, to hear a little song, read a good poem, see a fine picture, and, if it were possible, to speak a few reasonable words.—Johann Wolfgang Von Goethe (1749-1832), *William Meister's Apprenticeship," Book V, Chapter I*

> Look up, laugh loud, talk big, keep
> the color in your cheek and the fire in
> your eye, adorn your person, maintain
> your health, your beauty, and your animal
> spirits.—William Hazlitt

Everything is true, so long as it is not taken for anything more than it is.—Michael Oakeshott, 20th century political philosopher

Stubborn audacity is the last refuge of guilt.—Samuel Johnson: *Journey to the Western Islands of Scotland*

> Ladies touch babies like a banker touches gold.
> And outlaws touch ladies somewhere deep down in their soul.
> —Lee Clayton's song, *Ladies Love Outlaws*, as recorded by Waylon Jennings

My Brief Career As a 'Cycle-Riding Bootlegger

My first job as a newspaper reporter was in Manhattan, Kansas. It didn't pay much, but after a few months, I was beginning to save a little money. I'd never had a car and decided it made more sense to buy a brand new motorcycle for about $800 than to buy a used car for the same amount of money. So I got a blue Harley Davidson, and I've often since regretted that I talked myself into trading it in for a used car after I was married. But, by then, my wife was pregnant—and hauling a pregnant woman around on the buddy seat of a motorcycle didn't seem to be the right mode of transportation for her.

Anyway, her father hated motorcycles. It seems that he once owned one himself—and took a bad spill. So, while we were dating and even after we were married, we'd park the 'cycle down the street from her parents' house and walk the rest of the way, telling them that we'd arrived on the bus.

I was 19 or 20 years old then, and the man who sold it to me must have been all of 45. But at my age, 45 seemed very old to me, and I was surprised to learn that he, too, rode a 'cycle. "But," I said, "aren't you too old for that?"

He smiled. "I'll tell you something," he said. "No matter how old you get, in your mind you can always be as young as you were when you first went out on your own." Great advice. And it kept me thinking young all of my life—even after I'd passed 45 years!

The first day I had the Harley, I took two women from the newspaper staff for rides (long, slow rides since I had to put on 250 miles before I could take it up over 50 mph). My friends invited me to their apartment for supper, and we drank some wine. When I started home, I realized I was still a little woozy and of course it was the first time I'd ridden the thing at night. Well, at the first corner I met a cab and, trying to avoid a collision, I shot across the curb and through some bushes into someone's yard. I wasn't hurt and neither was the 'cycle but it was the last time—well, almost the last time—I ever drove it while drinking or after drinking.

There was the notable night when several of us newspaper-types were having a party. Everyone piled on my motorcycle and I drove about three miles through the heart of the city to the downtown bus depot at about 2 a.m., looking for something to eat. Luckily we didn't see a policeman—or none saw us. Two guys balanced on either side, with one foot on the footrest while they hung on with one hand, the other hand and leg flung out like circus acrobats. Three sat on the seat behind me, and another was a'straddle of the front fender and two more perched on the luggage rack. I wish I had a picture.

Kansas was a dry state then, and police could confiscate your vehicle if they found liquor in it. Heedless, I would make frequent trips north to the Kansas-Nebraska line to purchase booze, usually putting three fifths of whiskey in each of the two saddlebags. Most of the highway was gravel—tricky for bike riding—and once I met a car coming around a curve. There were only three tracks in the road, and the gravel was about six inches deep. As it happened, I was in the middle track—and so, of course, was one side of the approaching car. When the car driver didn't steer out of "my" track, I did at the last moment. The bike lost its footing and down I went. The headlight was dented somewhat, but my main concern was for the 6 bottles. They came through ok.

Another time, showing off downtown, I zoomed around the corner on brick cobblestone streets and leaned over too far. My footrest caught on one of the bricks and down I went. Embarrassed, I jumped up, righted the bike, and roared off—discovering later that the sole of my boot had been ripped almost entirely off.

Another embarrassment occurred while I was returning from a long trip. I ran out of gas a few miles from the nearest town—and was towed in by a kindly teenager on a motor scooter!

My "bootlegging" experience came in handy the time General Dwight D. Eisenhower came to Manhattan to speak at the college and visit his brother, Milton, who was president of Kansas State at the time. Ike was being talked-of as a presidential candidate, and a large contingent of bigtime reporters accompanied the general. I joined them in covering the speech (and got Ike's autograph on somebody's place card—not mine, because the reporters weren't invited to eat).

One of the visiting scribes wondered if I knew where to buy a bottle, and I said sure, and directed him to drive me to the bootlegger—in reality, to my own apartment. I told him he'd better wait in the car since "my friend" would be afraid to sell me a bottle with a stranger present. So I went up to my place, grabbed one of my bottles, and told the guy it cost $10, which he repaid to me. I think I had about $3.50 invested.

I try to remember that incident every time I—as a tourist—am ripped off while making a purchase.

Geezer Grins
THE SILLY SERGEANT

Count off, the sergeant said
And with a number from each man
You heard "one," in a high-pitched tone,
Then two, and three, and on to ten.

Wait a minute, the sergeant said.
Do all that once again.
Again squealed "one," then followed
Again the other bass-voiced men.

The sergeant looked at each in turn
Squinting in the morning sun
Starting first with number ten
Ending up with number one.

"Are you one?" he asked that man,
Then thought his career was through
When the soldier said in dulcet tones,
"Why yeth! Are you one too?"

> My duty toward my Neighbour is . . . to keep my hands
> from picking and stealing.
>
> *Book of Common Prayer*

The Great Watermelon Raid

I was born the year before the big stock market crash, but of course I missed it because I was too young. When the war in Europe began in 1939, I was 11 years old. I learned a new word from the radio: "inevitable." Because commentators frequently intoned: "War seems inevitable." They were right, of course. News commentators were right more often in those days.

Two of my older brothers joined the Army—one early in 1942 and the other in 1943. About that same time, I changed from attending a county high school where I lived in a dormitory during the week to a parochial school in another Nebraska town. There I first lived five days a week in a rented room, but later my father rented a vacant house where I did my own cooking and occasional housecleaning. About this time, to save himself from driving 30 miles twice a week to take me to school on Monday and pick me up on Fridays, my father bought a 1916 Model T Ford sedan for me. Now I can see that he perhaps trusted me more than he should have!

The car was purchased at auction for $50—selling cheap because its former owner had apparently gone insane, killed his parents, and committed suicide by jumping off of a bridge. After a few months with the car, I understood why.

But the Model T greatly enhanced my popularity at school—where the "country kids" (like me) were looked down upon by the "town kids." My car and the fact that I lived in town during the week and was already six feet tall—an asset to the basketball team—were my tickets to instant acceptance and some measure of popularity.

But this was wartime, and gasoline and tires were rationed. Finding good used tires was not much of a problem since there weren't that many Model T cars still in service. But securing gasoline without ration coupons—well, that required some ingenuity.

By accident one night, we discovered that a small amount of gasoline remained in the pump hoses of the town's three gas stations. Yes, the pumps were locked—but not the hoses. So, each night, we'd make the rounds, draining a pint or so of the precious fluid from each hose. The four-cylinder Ford didn't use much gas anyway, so our supply was sufficient for frequent nighttime trips to some nearby town where we had hopes of finding feminine companionship.

As if any young girl in her right mind would get into a car with a half-dozen half-drunk male high school students!

But my best-remembered adventure was the long night of the Great Watermelon Patch Raid. It happened this way.

And old hermit (probably 40 or 50 years old!) showed up in town regularly that fall with a wagonload of watermelons that he sold to local people. We had no spare change to buy watermelons, but it didn't take us long to find out exactly where his farm was located north of town.

So we waited until most people would be in bed, and made our rounds of the gas stations to re-fuel the Ford. A half-hour later we were standing in the midst of more melons than we'd ever seen. We were busy "thumping" them to find the ripe ones when suddenly the old man rose up from a hiding place, aiming a shotgun in our general direction, and shouted, "Now I've caught you, you thieving kids!"

There was no moon that night, and those of us farthest from the old man scattered like a flock of geese, leaving a luckless few to face the farmer's fury. Those of us who escaped headed for the car, perfectly willing to abandon the others.

But the old Model T would not start! We cranked and we cranked but not once did a cylinder fire. And so, there we were when our abandoned friends arrived, marching at the point of a gun. The farmer threatened to call the sheriff—my greatest fear, as the officer was related in some way to my family. So, we talked fast. Our story was that we had been told in town that the old man had more melons than he could possibly sell, and so he had announced that anyone who wanted some should come and take their pick.

Well, necessity is the mother of invention, they say. And there's nothing like a shotgun in the hands of a rightfully outraged melon grower to inspire a person to the most sincere form of lying. Finally, the farmer seemed to either accept our excuse or perhaps just decided that he'd given us a scare we'd never forget. He told us we could keep the three or four melons that some of us had not thought to drop during our flight.

Would he help me start my car? No, he said. That's your problem.

It happened that one of my uncles lived not too far away—a couple of miles—so we walked there and a cousin got out of bed to take us back on a tractor. Investigating, he found that the carburetor was filled with kerosene! Why? In our furtive raid on the gas stations, someone had mistakenly drained the kerosene pump's hose. No problem while the engine was running, but when we stopped to raid the melon patch, the heavier kerosene had settled to the bottom of the gravity-fed gas tank.

So we drained out the kerosene until we could smell gasoline again. My cousin pulled the car around with the tractor until the motor finally started, and we drove back to town.

There was just enough time to change clothes and go to school. The watermelons? We ate them on the ride back to town. And since that night I've never tried to steal a watermelon—or anything else!

Geezer Games
SHE AND ME

When she told me of her problems, I gave her solutions instead of sympathy.

When she talked to me, I heard what she had to say, and not why she was saying it.

When she reached out to touch me with her heart, I reached out to touch her with my hand.

And when she offered me her soul, I gave her my body.

But then, no man is perfect!

> A man loses his illusions first, his teeth second, and
> his follies last.
> —Helen Rowland

Climbing Social Ladders and Falling Down Stairs

I have never been much interested in climbing the social ladder. Spending long boring evenings making small talk with people with whom I would share limited interests could never compare in my mind to a quiet evening with a good book and some good music playing softly on the stereo.

But I was inspired once to make the effort when a fellow-worker told me that my employer's wife was overheard talking about me to one of her friends. "Oh, yes," she was quoted to me as saying. "Dennis is a good enough reporter, but, you know, he's a little lacking in the social graces."

Somehow, I knew right away what she meant—and also knew that she was right.

In addition to my newspaper job, I was employed as the part-time and slightly paid executive secretary of the town's Chamber of Commerce. I had moved there from a larger city where, also as a reporter, I'd become acquainted with that community's Chamber of Commerce secretary who since had gone on to become manager of the state organization. And so, needing a dinner speaker to inspire the members of my little group, I invited him—and he accepted.

It was my big chance to display my "social graces," and I was determined to make the most of it. So I invited our guest speaker and the local group's board of directors and their spouses (which included my publisher-boss and his wife) to a pre-dinner cocktail hour at my house.

My wife and I were anxious that everything go well, but didn't really know how to entertain. Oh, sure, we'd been to other cocktail parties, so we had at least a hazy idea.

To enhance the hors d'oeuvres, we bought an olive tree (which I realize now was intended to just sit on a table). But, anxious to be the perfect host, I picked up the tray on which the "tree" sat, and began making the rounds of our guests, offering "refills." Proving, indeed, that I was lacking in social graces.

Well, in this misguided act of hospitality, I swung the tray around and the plastic "tree" flew off the tray, hit the floor, bounced a couple of times, and came to rest at the feet of my employer's wife. And the olives rolled to every corner the living room!

Somehow, I recovered my aplomb in time to introduce the guest speaker later that evening, following the banquet. My introduction recounted his every activity since high school, and lasted only a few minutes less than his speech.

That banquet was held in the American Legion Hall, an organization of which I was also an officer. (Small town reporters get sucked in for responsibilities like this.)

And so on another occasion, I became involved in the Legion's plans to stage a "stag party" for out-of-towners who came there for the first weekend of the hunting season.

It was my first and only stag party! But I went along with the other officers of the Legion when they made plans for food, drinks, poker tables—and even some racy stag party movies that someone came up with. Did I say "racy?" Well, this was a few years ago and long before the inception the modern-day X-rated videos.

The spiciest film showed a negligee-clad woman stepping into a bathtub, allowing only commonly seen parts of her body to be shown as she sat down in the tub.

I looked around at the audience. Half of the men were on their feet—on tiptoes, actually—trying in vain to see over the side of that on-screen bathtub!

We had decided to charge a hefty admission price and supply free booze and snacks. And to take a cut of the pot with each hand of poker. Financially, this was a good move. And our visitors didn't drink too much, since they planned to be out early to begin hunting at daybreak.

But some of the local businessmen who also attended lacked the same restraint. And since the Legion Hall was located on the second floor, accessible only by a long narrow flight of stairs, some of the more-inebriated descended those stairs much more rapidly than they had originally ascended them!

One of them—a local grocer—did in fact fall and tumble end over end down the bottom half of the stairs. We all rushed to see if he was injured.

But he wasn't. He got to his feet, looked back up the stairs at the stricken face of one of his employees who had been trying to help him negotiate his exit, and said:

"That's all right, Bill. I know you didn't mean to push me."

Geezer Gibberish

SIGNS OF SOME TIMES
(Intended to be accompanied by illustrations of actual road signs)

NO U TURN me off, she cried.
I think you had better STOP.
CAUTION is called for now
Or else I'll call a cop!

DANGEROUS CURVES are what they are.
And if you don't respect it
They'll find your bloody body
At the very NEXT EXIT!

Bumper Stickers I've Never Seen:

BEWARE OF DRIVER'S GUIDE DOG
U DRIVE FASTER; I LIVE LONGER
AMERICA: LOVE IT OR LEAVE IT OR LET ME BE LONELY
HONK IF YOU *ARE* JESUS
WHEN I BOUGHT THIS STICKER A CAR WAS STUCK TO IT
LOWER THE AGE OF PUBERTY
SUPPORT WOMEN'S RIGHTS—HIRE A BROAD
IF YOU CAN READ THIS WE'RE IN A RADAR ZONE
SAVE GAS; STAY HOME
I WRITE; YOU WRONG
UP WITH THE NEEDY; DOWN WITH THE GREEDY
CHARITY: NO. BRIBES: YES

> "If the law supposes that," said Mr. Bumble,
> "the law is a ass, a idiot."
> —Charles Dickens, *Oliver Twist*

No Laws Against Laughter or Stupidity

Hoping to be more quickly accepted into the community, my wife and I began attending church when I took a job as reporter for a county seat weekly newspaper in Northwestern Kansas. The young adults class also had a Great Books Discussion group. We each bought a paperback set of books—classics like *The Prince* and some of the Greek philosophers—and we'd meet to discuss what we'd read. I liked to read and to talk, and enjoyed our sessions.

Though the group we became friends with a locally stationed highway patrolman—an asset to my job. This also helped me in my relationship with the county sheriff—almost to my undoing.

I was talking to the sheriff on the street one day when someone rushed up to tell him of a bad house fire a few miles from town. Let's go, I said, and we both jumped into my car and took off.

He kept telling me to speed it up, so I did. And then I remembered that I had an unsealed bottle of whiskey under the front seat on the passenger side; the side where the sheriff was sitting! Kansas was a dry state in those days, and if you were caught with an "open" bottle of liquor in your car, the court could take your car away from you and sell it.

There was nothing I could do, except make sure I didn't put on the brakes too quickly, because that would have surely flung the bottle out into the open, right between the sheriff's shoes.

My favorite law enforcement officer in that town was a little old deputy who mostly looked after the office. He told me a story once about a rape trial held there several years earlier.

"The woman was a big old tall rangy widow woman," he said, "and the defendant who was accused of raping her was a little sawed off runt of a man."

So the defense attorney was cross-examining her, and he asked her where this rape was supposed to have happened? In the hallway outside my apartment, she said. On the floor? asked the attorney. No, says she, up against the wall. Well, says the attorney, how in the world do you expect us to believe a little short guy like my client could rape a tall woman like yourself standing up against the wall?

She looked around the courtroom, and kind of batted her eyes and looked down at the floor and said, "Well, I guess a woman could kinda scrootch down a little!"

I never printed that story in the newspaper, but I guess it's all right to tell it to you now.

But my absolutely favorite "police" story dates from the 1970s when I was covering the Nashville music scene for a Chicago-based "fan magazine." The pay wasn't much, but the expense account was shaped like an accordion.

Anyway, I also took on a part-time role as operator of a beer tavern on Music Row, frequented mostly by would-be songwriters and singers. As I wrote elsewhere at the time, it was a favorite watering hole for "those who had tried and failed, and those who had failed to try." The customers were an interesting mixture, leavened at times when an honest-to-God successful songwriter would stop by. The regulars would immediately begin a "guitar-pull," an exhibition of creativity where as soon as one person finishes singing his/her song, others would "pull" the guitar out of the singer's hands, and begin warbling their own newest tunes.

This was in the days when hippies had not yet transformed themselves into yuppies, and a few hours of beer-drinking would sometimes wind up in a display of artistic difference—a fight, in other words.

And on this particular night, a songwriter went slightly berserk from too little success and too much beer and started dancing on the bar and scattering the free peanuts on the floor to mix with the sawdust. I'll call him "Preacher" because that's what he would do now and then on a Sunday morning when regret and guilt canceled his hangovers. Finally, we tired of his dance act and called the police.

They knew the way, so they arrived promptly, subdued the Preacher, and began leading him to the patrol car. One of Preacher's drinking buddies—I'll call him "Goatee" for his favored facial adornment—sought to intercede.

"If you're gonna take my friend to jail, you'll have to take me along with him," he told the cop. The officer gave him barely a glance before replying, "Okay, get your little ass in that car with him."

But, next morning, Goatee was waiting for me to unlock the door. "Some of my friends came down and put up bail for me," he explained.

I was curious. "What did the police charge you with?" I asked.

"Resisting arrest."

"What?" I said. "You didn't resist—in fact, you volunteered!"

"I know," he said. "That's what I told them. But they said they had to charge me with something . . . and there's no law against stupidity!"

Geezer Gaffes

DEATH ROW LAMENT
A prisoner sentenced to his death
Tried one last escape before dying.
Said he, First I was tried and found wanting;
Now I've been wanted, and found trying.

DOG GONE
Once I had a dog named Spot
And a cat that I called Hoover.
I miss my dog; it's the fault of my cat
'Cause she spilled my Spot remover!

SOCIAL SECURITY LAMENT
When I'd rather stay home in the evening
It's not because of the high prices.
The truth is, my dear, in my 65th year,
I'm suffering an energy crisis!

Candy is dandy / But liquor is quicker
—Ogden Nash, *Reflections on Ice-Breaking*

Going Out of My Head at Mardi Gras

"Mardi Gras" of course is French for "Fat Tuesday," and is celebrated most famously in New Orleans on the night before the beginning of Lent on "Ash Wednesday." In South America, it is called "Carnival," but the event is the same in intent—to have all the fun one can possibly enjoy before giving up such pleasures during the six weeks preceding Easter.

And so it was that six of us—three couples—decided to taste its pleasures one February. We made the trip down to the coast from Nashville in a van—not one of those luxury vans with chairs and beds. No, our transport was the stripped down version intended for use by workmen who needed the enclosed space to haul tools and supplies.

So we tossed a mattress in the back and a few blankets and a cooler filled with refreshments. And off we went!

And it was fun! The narrow streets of the French Quarter were filled with celebrants who were forced to occasionally give way to horse-mounted New Orleans policemen. No one was arrested for public drunkenness . . . the police seemed only interested in preventing or stopping the occasional fights.

We imbibed; we watched the parades and the women in our

party collected necks full of plastic beads and other trinkets thrown from the floats. But, eventually, the party cooled down, and we returned to our van to sleep during the few hours remaining before sunrise.

With six people, all more than a little tipsy, crammed into that van, I was sober enough to realize that I needed to find a safe place to store my eyeglasses. The cooler seemed a good choice, so I put them in it to keep company with our dwindled supply of beer.

Yes, beer. So of course a few hours later when it was still dark I awoke with the need to relieve myself at the nearby all-night gas station. But first—my glasses. Where? Then I remembered, opened the cooler, found them and put them on.

It was then I realized that I could no longer see clearly with my right eye! Still woozy from the night of partying, I was suddenly in a panic. I was going blind! I woke the others and finally someone had the presence of mind to turn on the interior light.

And then the five of them started pointing at me and laughing!

As it turned out, the right lens of my glasses had fallen out of the frame while they were in the cooler—maybe the ice made the lens shrink or something. No, I wasn't going blind after all! I popped the lens back into the frame, visited the gas station's restroom, and when I returned to the van, I found the other five asleep and taking up all of the space.

But I didn't care. I could see again!

> The fool doth think he is wise, but the wise man knows himself to be a fool.
> —Shakespeare: *As You Like It*

The Mazda and the Mechanic

Sometimes things happen that leave you shaking your head in disbelief.

My Mazda car started to shiver a bit when I first applied the brakes. A national chain with an auto repair department was close by my workplace and advertised brake jobs, so I called there to get a rough estimate. I told him what the symptoms were, and the service manager said, "Sounds like you need the rotors turned." Cost, he said: about $100.00.

"Bring it in tomorrow morning," he added, "and we'll check it out."

So I got up extra early and drove directly to the repair shop. I remembered the guy's name and asked for him. I told him again what the car was doing, and again he said, "Sounds like the rotors. We'll check and I'll call you at work."

He did, a few hours later, and said, "Sorry, we can't work on your brakes."

Why not? I asked.

"Problem is in the rotors. They need to be turned and we don't have the equipment to do that kind of work."

I was so dumbfounded that I said, "Well, as long as you have the car, give it an oil change and lube job."

Geezer Gripes

2 OUT OF 3 AIN'T BAD
Sometimes I'm late in arriving
But I'm not the malingering kind
So I always take my coffee breaks
And go home ahead of time!

HAG TO RICHES
She's accumulated a fortune
That'll fulfill her every needs.
From her last three husbands,
She's become rich by decrees!

MISTAKEN IDENTIFICATION
He was somewhat a smaller man
But that was not held against him.
And his wife was rather tall,
And fat where he was thin.

Yet no one would have noticed
If he hadn't said all his life:
"Hey, it's good to see you . . .
Have you met my *little* wife?"

LOVE MUCH

> Ye are better than all the ballads
> That were ever sung or said;
> For ye are the living poems,
> And all the rest are dead.

Henry Wadsworth Longfellow: *Children*

Geezer Genre

What will it take to make me happy?
    Oh, I don't know:
Money in the bank, and time to spend some;
A house in the country that I could call home.
    That would make me happy.

How will I know when I'm happy?
    Well, that is easy:
By the smile I'll see in my mirror and how I feel inside.
Mostly it will come easily when you are by my side.
    That's when I'll know that I'm happy.

Tony Robbins' Ultimate Success Formula:
Decide what you want. Can't hit a target that doesn't exist.
Take action. Take the small steps first to build confidence.
Figure out what's working for you, and drop what isn't.
Change your approach until you achieve what you want.

"The toughest thing about success is that you've got to keep on being a success. Talent is only a starting point in this business."— Irving Berlin, in *Theatre Arts*

> For the hand that rocks the cradle
> Is the hand that rules the world.
> —William Ross Wallace, *What Rules the World*

The Mother's Heart Is the Child's Schoolroom*

My mother died in a nursing home near Chicago, a lingering death at age 96 that I suspect—no, I am sure—she must have welcomed. Her final few years were under the care of her oldest daughter who took our mother into her home as a lingering illness began to mark the end of her long journey.

She was buried in the Nebraska community where she had raised her family and, despite the cold winter's day, and although she had not lived there for many years, her funeral was largely attended. Two of her eight children had preceded her in death.

I was the fifth of five sons, and enjoyed my "baby" status for about 10 or 12 years until the first of my three younger sisters was born.

A remarkable span of years did my mother enjoy—from the turn of the century when some Nebraska settlers were still residing in houses made of prairie sod, to the age of travel to the moon. She had traveled by horse and buggy, by automobile, and on a modern airliner.

My relationship with her was colored by the fact that my next older brother contracted polio when I was perhaps 3 or 4 years old. Since he required much of her attention, I have few early memories of her. Later, as the youngest, I became her "household assistant," and because of that, I learned to bake cookies and cake, and spent much of my boyhood time in her company and assisted in the care of my stricken brother.

It may be because of this that I grew up very unlike my older brothers. They tended to be argumentative, contentious. I learned to enjoy being by myself, and became an omnivorous reader. I read everything I could find—books, magazines, newspapers. The ideas and information I found in this form probably had much to do with my later inclination to a different career path and lifestyle than that of my siblings.

My mother was always my most severe critic. Her words would be: "Don't get too big for your britches." It might be that this admonition kept me from achieving as much as I could have, but it also could be that her warnings saved me from the possible error of trying to over-reach.

And, as the youngest son, I had the twin gifts of freedom and responsibility.

Freedom, because I was allowed to "live in town" while attending high school, and at 16 had my own car to drive home on the weekends.

Responsibility, because my brother with polio attended school in the same grades with me, and so I was his caretaker.

So I learned at an early age to connect the two—freedom, yes; but along with it came responsibility.

* * *

*Henry Ward Beecher

> The worst misfortune that can happen to an ordinary man is to have an extraordinary father.
> —Austin O'Malley

Things I Learned From My Father

I never borrowed any money from my father that I didn't pay back, and not over $100 total at that. Still, I am indebted to him in other ways. He wasn't old when he died—in his mid-50s, maybe. My memory of dates is not good. But I have never forgotten how I felt when I was told of his death.

In my early 20s then, I was not long married and with a very young daughter, and perhaps by contrast he seemed older then than he was. Or maybe it's that way with everyone, for the distance in years seems greater through the eyes of a child, like looking through the wrong end of a toy store telescope. That early image of our parents and other family members is difficult to see beyond as adults.

And since I obviously have a hazy impression of his age, I'm not sure now which of my other impressions of him are based on facts, and which have been distorted because I formed them through the young eyes/mind/emotions of my youth. It seems to me he was a very gentle person; maybe because that is how I prefer to think of myself.

He had a dog, Shep. We lived in the Nebraska Sandhills,

and we had lots of cattle, horses, dogs, and cats too. My mother couldn't turn away a cat, and apparently there was a feline network that spread the word, because a steady stream of homeless cats came to our place, and few were ever forced to leave. A favorite family story is about the time my father gathered up a sack full of chickens to sell at the local produce station. And, while he was at it, he also swooped up another sack—this time filled with some of our stray cats. Enroute to town, he stopped at the river bridge and dropped in the cat sack. Well, his punishment came when the produce station manager informed him that they weren't buying cats today. And my father realized he'd dropped the wrong sack into the river.

But back to Shep: he was my dad's dog. Maybe Shep wisely knew he had to choose between one adult or eight children, and took the road with the least traffic.

Shep grew old and feeble. It was summer and the hot dry winds blew out of the south, and he was sick. His ears became open sores on which flies feasted hungrily. Shep would ignore the flies. But if a child tried to brush the flies away, the old dog would growl and bare his teeth; only my dad could touch him. He wanted to put Shep out of his misery, but had to ask a visiting neighbor to do it for him.

Later, when I was old enough to have been taught how to use it, my dad let me use his single-barrel 12-gauge shotgun to go pheasant hunting. That's how he taught me the meaning of "take your best shot." The time elapsed while unloading, re-loading, aiming and firing meant that second shots were seldom a possibility. Pheasants move out at about 40 miles an hour and never come back to let you have a second try.

Now I'm coming to the real debt that I owe to my father. Not a big debt, you may say. But it looms large in my memory because it symbolizes a whole string of other similar favors that he did for me, probably without knowing what they would mean to me later.

Too young to go anywhere on my own, it was a great treat to be taken to the Cedar river for a cooling dip before supper after a hot Nebraska summer's day. Most days we would bathe in the small creek that ran through our land. But the creek wasn't very deep or wide and so the two-mile trip to the river was a big event.

I have a clear memory of one of those trips. I was pre-school, I am sure. The bridge on the road from which we gained access to the river seemed to rise mile-high, but a recent visit proves that it barely cleared the water by a few feet. Of course none of us wore swimming suits. I didn't even see a swimming suit until I was 17 years old, except those in the Sears catalog, and the ones I looked at there were in the girls' section. When we went swimming, we just took a quick look around, got out of our jeans, and jumped into the water.

Being very young, I was warned to stay in the shallow water, and that is where I was standing—in water up to my knees—when I heard the clip-clop of horses crossing the bridge. Naturally, I turned to see who it was. It was two women on horseback. They were from our valley too, but lived on the other side of the river.

Well, the two women looked at me, and I knew that they were looking at me, and I looked at them all the time their horses were walking across that old wood plank bridge. I was not the least bit concerned about or embarrassed by my nudity. Maybe I was even a little bit proud of it, because my older brothers were making such a big deal about covering their bodies with water.

"Leave him alone," my father told them. "He doesn't have anything to be ashamed of."

If my dad had ordered me to hide or pulled me down into the water that day to hide my innocent nakedness, it would have shamed me, and made me feel guilty. I might have lost that memory and retained only the feeling of shame.

Thanks dad!

Geezer Generalizations

BUSINESS COULD BE VERSE
Clever Wall street investor
Started dating his broker's sister.
But when the Dow fell in the well
She abruptly told him: Go to hell!

Inexperienced entrepreneur
Lost his dime down a sewer.
Tried his best; couldn't get it,
So his backers said just forget it.

A PEARL OF WISDOM
If you were a clam and I became sand
I'd turn into a pearl as big as your hand.
And give me to you? No! What the heck;
Everyone knows clams have no necks!

> We act as though comfort and luxury were the chief requirements of life, when all that we need to make us really happy is something to be enthusiastic about.
> –Charles Kingsley

Memories of Christmases Past

My Christmas memories focus on the annual School Christmas Program. I attended a one-room school, grades 1-8, and we started preparing for our "show" right after Thanksgiving.

The teacher would assign our parts. Usually each pupil would be in at least one play, and also would have to speak a "piece" or recitation. And, of course, all of us would be part of the chorus that always sang the same carols year after year. They weren't writing new Christmas songs in those days.

Our school had a stage across one end of the room, raised maybe 4 inches above the rest of the flooring. Other times this was where the teacher's desk was located, along with benches for whichever grade was having class. But now we'd move the teacher's desk off, and using a wire strung across the stage about 8 feet high, we'd hang heavy green burlap curtains—I can smell that burlap odor as I write this.

Other curtains made of bed sheets were used to screen off either side of the stage so "us kids" as we called ourselves would have some place to stay when we weren't on stage. Two of the bigger boys would be in charge of pulling the curtains open and shut for each presentation.

We always called the program date "that night," as in, "What are you going to wear that night?" And, when at last it arrived—usually the last Friday before Christmas—the school-age children just couldn't wait until the rest of the family was ready to ride in the car to the school. So we'd walk on ahead—one time even in a driving snowstorm that otherwise would keep me indoors these days, no doubt.

After the program, Santa would pop in and pass out "treats" to all the children, including those not old enough for school and maybe even a few who had graduated but were still in the community. The Christmas tree was always a locally-cut Cedar, about 8 or 9 feet high, it seems to me, but probably it was only 5 or 6 feet tall. It was decorated—as was our tree at home—with real candles that were burning with real flames. At school we also had a few ratty old decorations—paper bells that opened up, tinsel garlands, and the like. The younger pupils would make chains of paper strips glued into interlocking circles, and would string popcorn—which we also did at home. I don't remember any other "boughten" decorations, but maybe we had some colored glass balls. And probably an angel for the top of the tree.

And the evening concluded with a box lunch and pie social, with the ladies bringing the "eats" to be purchased at auction by the menfolks. Those furnished and purchased by the single men from single women of course brought the highest prices!

At home, we'd awaken Christmas morning to find that Santa had set the "good plates" out on the dining room table, and on each plate were pieces of my mother's homemade divinity candy, a few pieces of store-bought hard candy, and an orange. Each of us received one "big" present and a few lesser ones—the latter being mostly articles of clothing. My favorite was a lithographed tin service station, complete with a working hoist, gasoline pumps, and so on. I still have it today.

> Fortune knocks at every man's door once in a life, but in a good many cases, the man is in a neighboring saloon and does not hear her.
> —Mark Twain

Pick Your Parking Place With Care

I don't know exactly how I got started dating Lucy, but once started, it was a relationship that was hard to stop. I didn't have a car, and hadn't bought my motorcycle yet, but the newspaper I worked for as a reporter had a "staff car," an old and badly used Buick or something. Of course I wasn't supposed to drive it at nights except on business.

But my big chance came one weekend when the publisher's family took the top newspaper executives with them to some out-of-town event. That meant that no one was around to monitor the Buick, so I took Lucy driving in the country Sunday night. I turned into a hay meadow and we got kinda physical after which I got out to relieve my bladder and discovered to my horror that I'd driven into a well-plowed and barely green Kansas wheat field. The car had sunk to its axles just from standing there, and driving it out was a hopeless task.

So, we walked. We were about five miles from anyplace, and it was already near midnight, so there was no traffic and no houses where we might ask to use the telephone. We stopped at the first open gas station we came to which happened to have a wrecker service and I engaged the guy's services, sending Lucy home in a cab. Well, would you believe that the tow truck also got stuck? So the driver and I both walked back to town and he called another wrecker—this one equipped with an extra-long cable—and both vehicles were back on hard ground by about 4 a.m. My bosses were due back that morning so I barely had time to get the mud washed off the Buick and put it back in its parking space.

After that experience, Lucy and I often visited a nearby cemetery after dark. No one ever disturbed us there!

Geezer Gropings

To those who study her, Nature reveals herself as extraordinarily fertile and ingenious in devising *means*, but she has no *ends* which the human mind has been able to discover or comprehend.—Joseph Wood Krutch: *The Modern Temper*

We call that against nature which cometh against custom. But there is nothing, whatsoever it be, that is not according to nature.

Let us permit nature to have her way: she understands her business better than we do.—Montaigne: *Essays II & III*

Nature is not governed except by obeying her.—Francis Bacon: *The Advancement of Learning*

> There is not any memory with less satisfaction in it
> than the memory of some temptation we resisted.
> —James Branch Cabell: *Jurgen*

I Never Forget a Face!
(Now, What Was Your Name Again?)

I have a terrible memory for people's names. Always have. And I've always had a good excuse—but the truth is that I'm probably just too lazy. But what I claim is that because I spent many years as a newspaper reporter and editor, I trained myself to not rely on my memory for such details.

The famed Broadway producer Billy Rose used to say that seeing your name in the paper was like having your back scratched—but when it was printed over something you had written, it was like Miss America was doing the scratching!

To which I'd add—but only if your name is spelled correctly!

When I worked as a personal manager in Nashville's country music business, one of our busiest weeks was the annual "Fan Fair," when thousands of our most loyal "customers" converged on the city to enjoy afternoon and evening concerts of their favorite singers, presented by the various record labels. Between shows, the fans would seek out anyone who was anybody to secure autographs and take photos.

Every year, tour groups of country music fans from all over the U.S. and some from England and other countries would make the trip and, of course, we tried to give them as much as possible of what they wanted.

So it was that I happened to meet a delightful young lady from London who was shepherding a group of fans—mostly older ladies, it seemed—on a Nashville visit. And because the singer I represented was presenting a special nightclub show for his record company's visiting executives, I was able to take Miss Tour Guide to the show as my guest. She enjoyed the show, and I had a good time too.

A year later at the next Fan Fair time, I was working as a magazine journalist and happened to visit the office of my former employer.

"Oh, glad you stopped by," the receptionist told me. "A lady from England was in this morning and asked about you. She said she met you at Fan Fair last year and asked me to tell you that if you had time, she like you to stop by her motel." And she handed me a slip of paper with the woman's name, her room number, and the motel's name.

How nice that Miss Tour Guide remembered me, I thought, and went home to change to clothing appropriate for the evening ahead.

When I knocked on her motel door, an elderly woman opened the door.

"Hello!" I said. "Is Miss Johnson in?"

"I'm Miss Johnson," she said. "Aren't you Dennis Glaser? Remember, you were so nice to our tour group when we came last year and I would have been so disappointed if I hadn't gotten to see you again and tell you how much we all appreciated it."

It developed that "Miss Tour Leader" didn't make this trip, but Miss Johnson and I had a nice visit before she had to leave to attend that evening's concert. Me, I picked up a pizza on the way home. And vowed that I would never again forget which name goes with which face—but I still do.

> Marriage is that relation between man and woman in which the independence is equal, the dependence mutual and the obligation reciprocal.
> —Louis Kaufman Anspacher

You Gotta Pay the Piper—and the Judge, too!

My second marriage took place during our lunch hour—hers and mine. Actually, I've been married three times—but I don't really count the third one. It was over almost before it started—which would have been all right with me, except that she drove off in my Saab automobile. But that is another story.

So when No. 2 and I were married, we did it in a judge's office, over our lunch hour, as I said. We'd been living together, but for some reason I can't remember—maybe to please her parents—we decided to get married. And to do it with as little fuss and ceremony as possible.

It had been a long time since I was married the first time, and I had no idea how much to give the "judge" (actually he was just a magistrate—didn't even have to be a lawyer to hold that office in that state, though he was).

So I asked him how much was customary for his fee, and he said, "Whatever you want to give me is OK."

So I slipped him a $10, and he said, "Well, usually they give me at least $20." So I did. As it turned out, my wife and I had a friendly divorce some seven or eight years later. We are still friends, and I've always considered it $20 well spent. Especially compared with the cost of court-action divorce!

Geezer Get-Well Cards

I was sorry to get the news about your deafness
   . . . or hadn't you heard?

I was shocked to learn you'd gone blind
   . . . I hope there's someone there to read this to you!

Good luck on your upcoming cosmetic surgery
   . . . I'm sure you'll think it's an improvement

I'm so happy you're finally undergoing therapy
   . . . And everyone I've told about it felt the same way

Best wishes for a speedy recovery from your vasectomy
   . . . I'll always remember you as the man you once were

Sorry to hear you've got cancer
   . . . But at least now you know what's been eating you

> There is no greater nor keener pleasure than that of bodily love—and none which is more irrational.
> —Plato: *The Republic*

One in Time Can Last for Nine!

One Saturday night when I was waiting for my ship to leave the dock in Boston, another sailor and I wound up in Lynn, a nearby suburb, had a few beers, and then discovered we'd missed the last bus back to the city. We had our bus tickets, but no money or at least not enough for a hotel room.

So as you could in those days, we went to the police station where the night chief let us sleep in a cell, and then took us home with him the next morning for breakfast. It happened that he was a widower with a 17-year-old daughter and she and I got along well, and so I returned to Lynn often on nights when her dad was working.

As it turned out, she was the first girl I ever took to a hotel to spend the night, and boy, was that really a scary experience.

Since she was supposed to be staying overnight with a friend in Lynn, she couldn't pack a bag. And since I was afraid all the hotel rooms would be rented, I registered first with my sea bag-type luggage, and told the clerk that my "wife" would be in later.

But I met her at the bus depot so she wouldn't have to run the "risk" of asking the clerk for our room number. Well, things were different in those days at the tail end of World War II, and we expected a policeman or house detective to jump out from under the bed and arrest us at any minute.

I was only 18 myself, and with no previous overnight experience with a lover. But I had watched all the training films warning us to always use a condom. So I made sure that I got one from the pharmacist's mate before I left the ship.

Right, one condom. But I'd never needed more than one before! However, this night . . . well, what we did was rinse that one condom in the sink after each use, then wave it around in the air until it was dry enough to re-roll and re-apply!

Believe me when I say that in those days, I really didn't need the "time-out."

About two weeks later, I met another girl who lived in Boston (no expensive bus ride needed!) so I told the Lynn girl that I was shipping out. In a day or so, I came to my senses and dumped the new girl and called the first one and told her that a propeller had been damaged on my ship and we had to come back to Boston.

Later, when I reached my new station in Newfoundland, my Lynn lover kept writing to me, but I never replied—having other feminine interests at the time who were closer at hand.

Then, back in Boston on the way to St. Louis to receive my honorable discharge, I called Miss Lynn again and told her that our base had burned down and so I had lost her address. And that's why I couldn't answer her letters.

But, for some reason, she didn't believe me!

> A thing of beauty is a joy for ever;
> Its loveliness increases; it will never
> Pass into nothingness.
> —Keats, *Endymion*

The 'Capitol' Girl of the North Atlantic

Life can be boring when you are one of a handful of U. S. sailors stationed at a Coast Guard LORAN (Long Range Aid to Navigation) station on the farthest northeastern tip of Newfoundland during the waning days of World War II.

That's where I found myself in 1945-46, a Radioman 3/C fresh out of radio school in Atlantic City, N.J., a city even then abundantly supplied with pretty young women who were perhaps unwisely attracted to a man in uniform. Especially during the annual Miss America pageant!

Life was vastly different in Newfoundland, where a dog sled provided the most dependable transportation to the nearest village—Bonavista. Oh, there were a few pretty women there too, but there were also many hale and hearty fishermen who seemed to take a dim view when the women fraternized with the "yanks." But, of course, fraternize we did—whenever we had the chance.

Other times, we invented our own entertainment. For example, we conducted an on-going round-robin tournament involving, as I remember, shooting pool on a table with more bad spots than a teenager with acne; playing monopoly; and playing some kind of card game also—poker, most likely.

One night, when the cook was in town, we convinced his assistant to unlock the meat locker for us and helped ourselves to several of the steaks which otherwise were served only to the officers. We were frying the steaks with the kitchen window open to carry away the fumes when our lookout warned that the cook was approaching the camp.

The steaks were tossed through the open window into a nearby snow bank. After the cook had gone to bed, we tried to retrieve the meat—but it was gone! Eaten by the sled dogs. Who, despite the freezing temperatures, stayed night and day beneath that kitchen window for the next two or three weeks!

The Chief Radioman and I discovered that one of the Electronic Technician Mates was monitoring our transmissions on a spare receiver stored in another Quonset hut. Purpose, I suppose, was to get the "news" about any upcoming transfers before we radio operators had the opportunity to make these revelations.

It happened that the receiver they were using had a set of several frequency "coils"—each labeled for the shortwave broadcast bands that it covered. So the chief and I switched the nameplates around on all the coils so that no one could find the one that matched the frequency we were using. And, in case they ever did, we set up a coded signal we could give our base station in Labrador so that we both could jump from one band of frequencies to another on short notice, thus leaving our unauthorized auditors behind.

But the project that occupied most of our time that winter was our "Capitol Girl of the North Atlantic" contest. Chief Bill Turner (my boss) had started it just before I arrived, and I helped him complete it. We addressed letters to "The Leading Newspaper" in each state capitol city in the U.S., asking their help in publicizing our beauty contest. Girls had to be 18 or over, single, and write a letter to us telling all about themselves and enclosing two pictures, including one of her in a bathing suit.

Well, nearly all 48 newspapers went along with us, and soon the letters began to pour in—probably 2,000 or 3,000 in all. At that point we had to ask everyone on the base to help, and we set up a rating system for each girl. Guys from each state got to pick the winner from their state, and the other state winners were based on a majority vote. Only we didn't call them "state" winners—as far as each winning girl was concerned, she and only she was the "Capitol Girl of the North Atlantic," according to a "news release" we mailed to her hometown paper.

My last official act in connection with the contest was to type up a complete list of "cream" of the entries from each state, with copies for each of us to use when we returned to the states. For my part, I never made it to a state capitol during those days, but I did keep my copy of the list—just in case.

The photos . . . I don't know what became of them. But I do remember that they were posted in the rec hall while I was there, and, like the letters, were great morale boosters during those long cold evenings!

Geezer Gifts

Natural Predators; Obvious Victims
Bowling ball, chicken's egg
Tall trees, low-flying aircraft
Bare feet, burrs and stickers
Juicy peach, clean shirt
Television, entertainment
Credit cards, savings accounts
Stock market, small investors
Law, order
Justice, mercy
Education, experience
Marriage, romance
Rainy days, summer weekends
Herpes, happiness
Sitting, thinking
Death, life,
Greed, need
Fleas, dogs
Spaghetti sauce, white table cloth

> A love-match is generally a failure and a money-match is always a mistake. The heroes, the saints and sages—they are those who face the world alone.
> —George Norman Douglas: *South Wind*

The Gold-Digger Problem

She was beautiful, this co-worker I'll call Sambia. Her's was that dark-skinned, exotic and flashing-eyes beauty common to some young women with Mid-Eastern antecedents. Most of the time I knew her, I was not in a relationship. Nevertheless, I never attempted to move beyond friendship with Sambia.

There were good reasons for my hesitancy to ask her for a date. First of all, I never liked to get involved with co-workers. Although she was a graphic artist and I was an advertising copywriter, our jobs overlapped enough to make me want to avoid the inevitable fallout should we try becoming a couple, but then fail. Also, her ex-husband was employed by the same company, and I noticed that he took care to avoid unnecessary contact with her. I supposed he had good reason.

But, then, truthfully, Sambia was usually dating someone else. And, because she considered me a good listener (which I am), she often discussed her current love affairs with me, seeking advice that she of course never followed. But then, who does?

It was her need to discuss her relationships with me that caused me to hear her side of this story.

Sambia's then-current boyfriend—let's call him Ken—worked

as a middle manager for a large retail store group and probably earned twice as much as his girl friend. Thinking perhaps that a "budget" was some type of pet bird, she frequently would outspend her paycheck, and as if it were her due, immediately turn to Ken for a financial supplement.

But finally, she went too far. I don't remember what she purchased—likely some expensive item of clothing—but it caused her to ask Ken once again for money. He objected. She insisted. He resisted. She, as usual, overcame.

But he didn't make it easy for her. She, of course, told me all about it. To my misfortune, she always told me everything about everything!

Ken gave her several checks that added up to the exact amount she needed. But instead of writing her name on each check, he instead wrote such things as "Miss Spendthrift," "Ms Overpriced," "Mrs. Moneygrubber," and "Mathematically-Impaired." I think there were 10 or 12 such checks in all, each with an unflattering payee's name written in similar fashion.

And Sambia . . . well, Ken's little joke was that he knew that in order for her to cash or deposit his checks at the bank, Sambia would have to endorse each one with her name preceded by the title he had awarded to her on each check.

And she did. But not long after that, the relationship was over.

> Anger is a brief madness and, unchecked, becomes
> protracted madness, bringing shame and even death.
> —Petrarch: *Sonetti sopra, Vari Argomenti*

A Martyr to Safe Sex?

Old Will never did like me, and I'm not sure why. But I always had my suspicions.

1. I arrived in town in the midst of the second Eisenhower presidential election campaign—and Old Will accused me of giving more space to Ike on page 1 of my newspaper than I gave to his Democrat opponent, Adali Stevenson. Maybe I did, one day or another, but then the next day, Stevenson would make more news, and deserve more coverage.

2. Will was about the same age as the publisher of my competitor newspaper, who also was an out-loud Democrat. Me, I was just a young squirt by comparison, with no political affiliation.

3. Both Will and my competitor were "old-timers" in town and I was just a "newcomer."

Will was a dealer for a popular brand of tires at his highway filling station—and I knew from experience that the tire company had a good cooperative advertising program, paying half and sometimes more for local ads. Try as I might to convince Will to place at least some of this advertising in my newspaper, Will always ran his tire ads in the other paper. Finally, I quit calling on him.

Will died before I left that town. Of a heart attack. Suffered when his retail gasoline franchise zone manager told Will he'd have to get rid of the condom machines in the men's restroom. The machines were an important source of tax-free cash income to Will—and he greeted this news with a fit of anger, and dropped dead on the spot. Or so I was told: "I know not what the truth may be, but tell the story as it was told to me."

So did Will die a martyr to safe sex, a legend before his time?

Or was it just his greed that killed the old coot?

One more thing:

A couple of years before Will died, his biggest local competitor in the tire business steered me to what became a major sideline business for my newspaper printing plant—the design, manufacture, and mailing of millions of farm tire circulars all over the U.S. for another brand of tires. This led to a contract with a second major tire manufacturer—but neither one was the brand Will used to sell.

Geezer Giggles

TAVERN ADVISORY FOR MEN
Just tell the ladies
What they want to hear
And you'll save the cost
Of buying them beer.

REASONS FOR LIVING
You'll find new reasons
For staying alive
When once you pass
Age sixty-five!

ROYALTY REDUX
Antecedents hinted,
Accent blighty:
Some English think
They're the almighty!

Geezer Goodies

Love starts with "L" but soon moves on to "Oh!"

Children, tests have shown, learn how to experience love in their first or second year . . . and how to feel shame in their fourth year. Society, unfortunately, seems dedicated to reducing the interval.

If "love makes the world go 'round," lots of people get a free ride.

The word Love sounds better than Hate—and makes you feel better too.

In a Lou Harris survey asking people to name the guiding principle in their lives, the Golden Rule was the most popular answer. The one I like best ranked near the bottom of the top 10: "Someone to love, something to do, and something to look forward to."

If someone demands that you give him or her your love, likely he or she has none of his or her own to give to you.

Like love, sympathy is something you give, not seek.

The best way to let others know how you feel is to SHOW them instead of trying to TELL them how you want them to *think* that you feel.

BEST FRIENDS

> I think I could turn and live with animals, they are so placid and self-contain'd.
> I stand and look at them long and long.
> They do not sweat and whine about their condition.
> They do not lie awake in the dark and weep for their sins.
> They do not make me sick discussing their duty to God.
> Not one is dissatisfied, not one is demented with the mania of owning things.
> Not one kneels to another, nor to his kind that lived thousands of years ago.
> Not one is respectable or unhappy over the whole earth.

Walt Whitman: *Song of Myself*

Geezer Guff

If a woman has to choose between catching a fly ball and saving an infant's life, she will choose to save the infant's life without even considering if there are men on base.—Dave Barry

If most of us are ashamed of shabby clothes and shoddy furniture, let us be more ashamed of shabby ideas and shoddy philosophies.—Albert Einstein

People who live in stone houses should not throw glasses.

Too much of a good thing can be wonderful.—Mae West

To enjoy enduring success we should travel a litttle in advance of the world.—John McDonald

The demands on our creative abilities have doubled in every generation.—Peter F. Drucker

I start where the last man left off.—Thomas Edison

Every problem contains the seed of its own solution.—Norman Vincent Peale

If you think you can or can't do something . . . you're probably right.—Henry Ford

> I would like, to begin with, to say that though parents, husbands, children, lovers and friends are all very well, they are not dogs. In my day and turn, having been each of the above—except that instead of husbands I was wives—I know what I am talking about, and am well acquainted with the ups and downs, the daily ups and downs, the sometimes almost hourly ones in the thin-skinned, which seem inevitably to accompany human loves.
> Dogs are free from these fluctuations. Once they love, they love steadily, unchangingly, until their last breath. That is how I like to be loved.
> Therefore, I will write of dogs.
> —Elizabeth von Arnim

A Gift of Love from My Dog Freckles

When I lived in or around Nashville, Tennessee, there were three things I would count on when May gave way to June:

1. It would rain during "Summer Lights," a big downtown street fair that was held for the local people the weekend before the country music industry's Fan Fair marks the annual renewal of the tourist season.

2. It would turn hot-hot-hot during Fan Fair. Up until then,

the weather could get really regressive; warm days make you enjoy working in the garden while the cool nights will send you digging in the closet for the sweaters you packed away a few weeks earlier. But, when Fan Fair arrived the first week in June, the mercury zoomed into the 90s . . . and stayed there. It was the area's way of getting even with the 25,000 tourists who clogged the interstates and streets with cars, campers, and house trailers carrying guys wearing baseball caps and overweight women dressed in shorts or pants that are a bit too tight.

    3. If you lived on a farm and were trying to put up the first cutting of hay, those scattered afternoon showers caused by the season's last cold front from the north meeting the northerly flow of hot, moist air from the south would devil you every time you would try to cut the grass. And be followed by superheated high humidity when you tried to complete the hay harvest.

    I had only about 6 or 7 acres of meadowland—seeded to a mixture of fescue and clover—with some Johnson grass and a sprinkling of weeds—and mostly carefully cleared of rocks by a previous owner and kept that way by me. And, since I used the hay for garden mulch and not for livestock feed, I couldn't afford the usual mechanized routine of cut, rake, and bale. Instead, I used my two-wheel walk-behind sickle mower with a 4-ft. blade, a pitchfork, and my mini-pickup truck. Let me explain.

    I could cut the whole field in a couple of days. But since it took me another week at least to windrow, buck, and haul, I usually spent about an hour a day cutting, and the rest of that day harvesting.

    The mower left a more-or-less windrow—actually, it created a clear strip about 12 inches wide between the two-foot-wide strips of hay. The meadow was mostly on a gradual hillside, so I worked with my pitchfork up and back down the hill, combining three to five rows of hay into one; three to five depending on how heavy the grass was at that particular place. Took me, oh, 20 minutes or so to use my pitchfork to combine the windrows up and back down the hillside, and another 10 minutes to bunch up the hay in rows far enough apart so my pickup would fit in between.

It's a good long walk from the house, so I always drove out, windrowed and bunched until I got hot and tired, then loaded up the truck as high as I could reach, and hauled it back to the garden. The year I'm writing about, I was stacking the hay in an area I would add to my garden the next year. My method was to plant part of my old garden area in buckwheat in the fall, till it under, and then sow it to crimson clover to add nitrogen and compost. The rest of the garden would still be covered with hay mulch which I'd till under late in the fall, and then re-mulch until spring—at which time I'd drag the mulch off, till again, plant, and then re-mulch.

In addition to adding organic matter to my heavy clay soil, the mulch helped keep moisture from evaporating. The added organic matter, on the other hand, makes the soil more friable, which means that the clay molecules are separated enough to increase the soil's moisture-holding qualities. I'd used mulch for 5 or 6 years, and each year the soil got a little darker, and the darkness went a little deeper and more earthworms would appear—a sign of healthy soil.

And so it was on a hot day in June 1993. My pickup was parked at the top of the hill, and the temperature was about 92 degrees, and I'd been windrowing and bucking for over an hour and was more than ready to go sit on the porch and put my body around a couple of big glasses of cold iced tea—otherwise known as the house wine of the south.

My dog Freckles was old, a little crippled in the joints, and almost deaf. She was so deaf, in fact, that when I called her to eat, I would have to wait until I caught her eye, then motion to her. Sometimes when I'd walk out of the house and let the screen door slam without realizing Freckles was around, she'd jump up out of a sound sleep when she heard the noise, and then look at me kind of sheepishly.

But wherever I went on the farm, Freckles went. Up until a

year earlier, when old age began to get to her, she would range out on either side of me, hunting for rabbits or mice or whatever she could scare up. One time a snake surprised her, and she jumped vertically into the air, like the dog in "Peanuts." But then she began just trailing after me, and finding a comfortable place to rest when I reached a work site—a spot out of the wind in the winter and shaded in the summer.

And so this day, when I reached the pickup, she was dozing in its shade, and I stopped to kneel down beside her because she always needed lots of love and also to check her ears, neck, and back for ticks. There were a few—not as many as the last year. And after I'd dispatched the pests, I paused for a few moments to rub her back and the top of her head between the ears—the latter a place where dogs especially appreciate receiving attention since it is one spot that's hard for them to reach effectively. Then, I started moving the truck down the hill, stopping between every four piles of hay, checking the rear-view mirrors for her location. As usual, I didn't bother to start the motor; just pushed in on the clutch and let the truck roll downhill.

After pitching the hay in, I looked for her again, and saw her snoozing on the shady side of a pile of hay halfway down the hill. So I released the brake and pushed in on the clutch to coast the few feet to the next four piles. I noticed Freckles was still in the same spot when I went back around on the driver's side to finish loading. I got in, released the brake and clutch again, and the truck started to roll. Then I heard a horrible thump and her anguished yelp.

I knew immediately what had happened. She'd moved to the shade under the truck to be near me. I set the brakes and put the truck back into gear, and jumped out. Just as I got to the back of the truck, Freckles came rushing around to meet me—and fell on her side at my feet. I talked to her, manufacturing a reassuring tone of voice that I didn't feel, and felt her body for broken bones. There was no blood, but she wasn't making a sound, and by then her pupils had rolled back and she was breathing only slightly if at all.

The truck was piled high with hay, so I started unloading enough so I could put her in and take her back to the house. But before I could finish, she was gone. Probably of internal injuries.

I drove back to the house, unloaded the hay, and had a cup of coffee—iced tea didn't seem strong enough. By then I knew what I had to do, and got a shovel from the garage. Back out in the meadow, the ground was hard and dry, and full of palm-sized stones. But the hard work was therapeutic in a way. I dug and dug until I was sure that the hole was big enough, then placed her body in the grave so she was lying on her stomach, covered it with a layer of clover hay, and completed the task. A day or two earlier, while mowing, I had spotted a patch of wild daisies. When I had reached the flowers, I had changed course enough to leave standing a row of them, maybe a foot wide and three feet long.

So after the next time it rained, I transplanted them on both sides of Freckles' grave so I would always know where it is.

* * *

I am not a person who gives animals human qualities. For example, I probably would not have taken Freckles to a veterinarian for surgery, drugs, or other life-saving measures. I think that animals are born, live, and die. If in their world surgery and drugs and so on were supposed to exist, then I think that they would have worked that out for themselves.

But I respect animals, and had Freckles been in misery, I would have not allowed her to suffer needlessly.

Further, when other life forms become a part of my life and then leave it—as did my parrot Kris and this dog Freckles—I try my best to discover the lesson they offered me the opportunity to learn.

Kris, for example, taught me about freedom. As her human namesake, Kris Kristofferson, wrote in a song: "Lord, help me to carry / the burden of freedom / and give me the courage / to be what I am. / And when I am wounded / by those who condemn me / Lord help me forgive them; / they don't understand."

And what was the lesson left by Freckles? Well, Freckles gave me the chance to realize that what I really value in life are "feelings." Some examples:

I don't want money; I want the *feeling* of security that having some money in the bank gives me.

I don't want this or that person to love me; I want to *feel* that I love them and am loved by them.

And that is what is really behind my own little six-word prayer: Life, Love, Peace, Prosperity, Health, Happiness.

Those six words represent ways I want to feel, not "things" that someone else has managed to manipulate me into desiring. And it is my wish for you that this little story about a dog will help you understand how important feelings should be in your own life.

That would be one more gift of love from my dog Freckles.

> No man can lose what he never had.
> —Izaak Walton: *The Compleat Angler*

Freedom: Not Just Another Word to a Parrot

I never knew how old Kris was. That's the kind of relationship we had. Kris and I didn't pry into each other's past; we accepted one another as we were—warts, wattles, hooked beaks, and all.

Maybe you've noticed I have not used a personal pronoun for Kris. That's because I have no idea whether Kris was male or female. I guess only another parrot would know for sure. But I always suspected Kris was a female; certainly she was very jealous of human females. So I'll refer to her thus, for simplicity's sake.

Her ambiguous gender was only partially responsible for her name; "Kris" could be male or female. But I named her after Kris Kristofferson, one of my favorite songwriters. Who wrote a somewhat famous and slightly existential line in his song, *Me and Bobbie McGee*:

"Freedom's just another word for nothing left to lose, and nothing ain't worth nothing if it's free."

When I was a child on the southeastern edge of the Nebraska Sandhills, one of our neighbors had a parrot, said to be over 40 years old, and I grew up with a secret desire to have one too.

After I was married, I started hanging out in the pet department when I'd accompany my wife shopping. I'd check out the parrots, and price them, and consider the cost of cages, food, and so on. Later, Willie Nelson would warn in a song: "Be careful when you're dreaming, or soon your dreams will be dreaming you."

One day back in the 1960s, I told my wife that I'd seen a reasonably good-looking parrot for only $29.95, I think it was. "Why don't you buy it?" she asked. Well, you know how it is when there is something you've always wanted, and then finally you can have it . . . and you want to have it, but you also want to keep on wanting it. Because you are so accustomed to the desire, you almost regret giving up the wanting in exchange for the having. But she had me cornered, and so I decided that, yes, I would buy a parrot.

Next the decision was which one. For there were two of the birds in the pet store—both of a species I later learned was called Mexican Redheads. One was well-behaved; the other an aggressive bully bird who was always pushing the "nice" parrot around. So I bought the aggressive one. Later I wondered whether I shouldn't have bought the wimp.

When I got the parrot home and out of the box and put her into the cage . . . well, she must have been scared out her wits! For about a week, all she did was stand on a perch in the cage. Seldom moved, except to eat and drink. Hardly uttered a squawk, let alone made any conversation.

After a few days, I moved the cage near a window in the den. It was next to the telephone, which rang a lot in those days. And so one day when I walked into the den to answer the ringing phone, the parrot said "Hello!" It was quite a surprise, as I hadn't really tried to teach her anything, but I guess Kris picked up the word from hearing the phone answered several times a day. Anyway, that was her first word. But not her last.

Next was "How are you?" And that probably was because when Kris said "hello," I would reply, "How are you?" Then, in whatever order, came "What's the matter?" "Thank you," and

"OK, Kris." I tried but failed to teach her to say, "Birds can't talk." I thought it would be her perfect retort to most people's initial question to the parrot: "Do you talk?"

I'd read a couple of books about parrots, and one advised teaching it to perch on your arm by first training the bird to step onto your finger. Just open the cage door, and put your finger in next to the perch, said the book, and the parrot will step onto your finger. Not Kris. She leaned down and bit my finger. So I bought a pair of heavy leather work gloves. She still bit my finger—and that bolt-cutter beak could chomp hard enough to draw blood even when biting through the leather. Her technique was to first clamp down, then grind her upper beak back and forth for maximum effect.

Finally, she learned to step onto a stick held in my hand, and I could even stroke her upper beak or sometimes the top of her head as long as she was standing on the stick and away from the cage. But the cage was her hometown territory, boy, and you'd better not lay a hand or glove on Kris when she was defending herself in or on her own little kingdom.

From the outset, I had second thoughts about the idea of keeping the bird locked up in a cage. You know, most pets are free to roam about—to some extent, at least. (Only fish and snakes also are closely confined.) Much of the time I left the cage gate open so Kris was free to climb up on top of her cage and sometimes, when frightened or just bored, she would take off and fly around the room. Her flying skills were always a little awkward, and her landings were usually hilarious when attempted any place except on the cage.

I was advised to get her wings clipped—but didn't because I felt her ability to fly might be her only defense from attack by a dog or cat. (And cats especially harbor a hate for birds. Once when I had Kris's cage hanging out in the back yard, I found a neighborhood cat literally hanging by a single toenail from the cage bottom, having tried unsuccessfully to leap four feet from the ground to the suspended cage.)

All the years she lived with me, Kris was her own self. She only occasionally would let me touch her, but it always had to be her decision—not mine. The closest thing to affection came when another animal—like a dog—was in the house. Kris would claim her prior rights to my attention by squawking at me. And if out of the cage, which she mostly was, she would fly at me, sometimes even grabbing my hair with her claws as she fluttered above my head. I spilled many a cup of coffee when she'd seemingly arise from a sound early morning sleep to dive bomb me as I was leaving for work when there was a dog in the house. Once the visiting dog was gone, however, she'd settle back into her old ways.

As the years moved on, and as I moved on with them, Kris became an enduring presence in my life . . . the one thing constant when everything else would change—wives, cities, homes, cars. When I went on a car trip, Kris would ride with me in her cage atop a piece of luggage in the front passenger seat—thus raised high enough so she could see out through the windshield and windows. If I spent the night in a motel, she'd stay there with me, even if I had to sometimes smuggle her in with something covering the cage.

Music affected her. Generally speaking, she preferred pop and country music to rock and gospel, and liked low-range voices better than sopranos. Waylon Jennings she would enjoy; Dolly Parton's high-pitched voice would bring a quick and vocal objection. Sometimes she would go into what I called her Ray Charles act—spreading her tail feathers, arching out her wings, stiffening her neck, extending her beak, and rhythmically rocking back and forth a few inches from one end of a perch to another.

Birds molt, and Kris would lose some of her feathers from time to time. If there was a seasonal schedule, I never figured out what it was. But I could always tell when the molting process was nearly complete; Kris would lose most of the red splotch of short topknot feathers on her head—which would then grow back in a matter of a few days. Mostly, her other feathers were green with a little yellow and a touch of red on her wings plus the red pate which gave her the "Mexican Redhead" name.

When Kris stretched, she would extend one wing and matching leg, and then the other pair. My wife figured Kris was showing off those pretty red feathers, and would sound the wolf whistle—and Kris seemed to appreciate the attention. Between the two of them, she and Kris worked out a routine of whistling, with one starting a two-part whistle sequence and the other one finishing it. Kris could handle either role: whistle starter, or whistle ender.

When angry, or excited, and often at sunset, the bird could produce an ear-piercing shriek or cry—usually three loud blasts followed by four "caws": whistle, whistle, whistle, caw, caw, caw, caw. That meant Kris definitely wanted something—attention, probably.

For she did like attention, Kris did. More and more as the years went on. Until finally, she could not abide being alone in a room if anyone else was in the house. I supposed that Kris was under the impression that when I left the room she was in, then surely I had gone to the kitchen to get her something to eat. And, on reflection, I can understand that anyone—any being, I guess that should be—that had to spend its life either in or atop a tiny cage and who didn't have the ability to seek her own food would indeed begin to think that life centered precisely on what there was to eat, and when she would get to eat it.

Kris preferred sunflower seeds as a staple diet, cleverly cracking them with those powerful beak-jaws, and using her worm-looking tongue to neatly separate the seed from the shell. She was a social eater, preferring to dine when others were eating, or at least when others were around. She had varied, and changing, tastes. Bits of fruit, buttered, jellied, or peanut-buttered bread, cookies, cheese crackers (but not crackers as in "Polly want a cracker?") She became especially fond of noodles, macaroni, and spaghetti. And Kris would eat meat, fish, or poultry—but I didn't intentionally give her any . . . fearing, somehow, that it would be a mistake to turn her toward the carnivorous.

Like any caged animal, she didn't like to have things poked at her—a defense reaction, no doubt. And that included fingers that might be stuck innocently through the cage bars while putting food in her dish, or changing her drinking water.

Once, when I took her to my office at the record company where I was employed then, the boss brought his big dog—I forget the breed, but it was one of those b-i-g ones—to work that day. The dog trotted into my office with that self-assurance big dogs seem to exude, went directly to Kris's cage, and stuck his big black nose right between two of the cage wires. Kris showed no signs of alarm . . . just calmly leaned forward, stretching her neck a bit to reach her goal, and clamped that viselike beak on the dog's honker. The dog yelped in total surprise, backed off, and left my office without another word. And never returned.

Reminds me of Mark Twain's comment about cats and hot stoves. "When a cat jumps on a hot stove," he wrote, "that cat will never jump on another hot stove again. Nor on a cold stove!"

Parrots spend a lot of time grooming, like all birds. Those thousands of feathers each must be cared for, and excessive amounts of tiny white pinfeathers have to be plucked out and discarded to float about the room, alighting on TV screens, clothing, furniture, carpet, and elsewhere.

And, from time to time, Kris would decide she needed a bath before I reached the same decision. She would attempt to climb into her drinking water—a container about three inches by two inches and maybe one and a half inches deep—and "splash" around. That was my clue that it was time to take the caged bird outside and gently hose her—and the cage—clean. In winter or where no outdoor hose was available, I'd put the cage in the bathtub and turn on the shower.

Cage cleaning was not a pleasant task (the phrase "you dirty bird" originated from some truth, let me assure you). After I found a duplicate cage in a second hand store, I usually alternated the two since it was easier for me to scrub one down while Kris occupied the other one.

When I purchased a home in the country but before I moved there, I began taking Kris along when I planned to stay at the farm for the weekend. And, of course, it was a perfect place to bathe the bird and cage. And that indeed was my task on the day of Kris's great flight to freedom.

Since a dog had come with the farm, and since Kris disliked dogs almost as much as she seemed to fear cats, I usually kept the bird locked in her cage even while inside the farmhouse. For one thing the screen doors didn't have spring closers, and sometimes tried to stand open. For another thing, the dog occasionally managed to follow me into the house.

So I picked up the cage with the bird inside and toted them outside to where the garden hose was connected, and put the cage on the ground. As I started to pick up the hose, Kris (and I) realized that the cage door was OPEN, and she rapidly clambered onto the top, using beak and feet with equal facility in the way parrots do. "Get back in," I admonished her firmly, using a tone of voice that would sometimes get her to obey. At the same time, I reached for my handkerchief, knowing that Kris usually would move away from any attempt to cover her with a cloth, usually seeking shelter back in her cage. But not this time.

This time, she literally rose to the occasion, and flapped away halfway to the top of the nearest tree, and perched on a branch. Now, the possibility that Kris might someday escape had crossed my mind, and I had once read that two principles would apply: (1) Caged birds are likely to return to their cage, having come to think of it as a secure place. (2) Best way to get a bird out of a tree is to squirt water on it, because birds find it hard to fly with wet feathers (tame birds, that is; I was taught as a child that putting salt on a wild bird's tail was the recommended method for catching them).

So I moved the cage to where Kris could see it easily, and turned on the hose. The stream from my low-pressure water system reached only halfway to the perch Kris had selected. Well, I knew she loved grapes, and that my grapes were ripening, so I went down to the grape arbor and selected a half-dozen purple ones and put them in the cage's food container. Then I left the scene for a while, figuring that if I was not in sight (and I'd locked the dog in the house), the bird was more likely to return to its brass-wire nest.

Didn't work, but while I was gone Kris did move from tree no. 1 to tree no. 2, the latter being a bit toward the direction I had gone. So I suspected that she had given some thought at least to following me. Still the bird wouldn't budge, and finally it was time to go back to the city, and I did, albeit reluctantly, leaving the cage up high, but in plain sight. This was late on a Sunday evening, and I had things I had to do before going to work the next morning.

Monday I left work early and drove back to the farm, both to see if the bird was still there, and also to get a half-bushel of ripening tomatoes I had forgotten when I left Sunday. Well, Kris was still there, all right. Sitting on the very same tree limb, far as I could tell. I checked the cage. Some of the water seemed to be gone, and half of the grapes had been chewed up and skins dropped on the cage floor. So either Kris had flown down and dined—or other birds had, since I had fastened the cage high up on the side of the porch so the dog—and other animals—couldn't get to it.

Kris would whistle at me, and make other noises to let me know that she knew I was there. And she would cock her head to one side and look at me when I looked up at her. But she wouldn't talk. Well, I thought, if I could get her to move, maybe she would fly back to the cage. So I started chucking small rocks in her direction—not trying to hit her, but just to make enough noise zipping through the tree branches and leaves to get her attention. No response. Then I picked up a small tree branch lying on the ground and tossed it up into the tree. That did the trick.

Kris squawked once in reproach and took off—but in the wrong direction. She headed due south toward the meadow, then—high in the sky—she wheeled around in a big circle, headed toward the tall trees near the barn that is about 200 yards north of the house. I couldn't find her again, though I had thought I heard her calling somewhere down by the barn. I left the cage where it was, thinking that if she decided to come back, she'd be more likely to find the cage where she'd left it than anywhere else.

I drove back to the city with the memory etched in my mind's eye of Kris flying high in the air, wings smoothly working, moving quickly across the clouds. Flying. Just like a bird. Flying as free as a bird.

Kristofferson's song echoed in my mind: "Freedom's just another word for nothing left to lose."

Geezer Gibes

The quality of an organization can never exceed the quality of the minds that make it up.—Harold R. McAlindon

Chance favors the prepared mind.—Louis Pasteur

The most valuable 100 people to bring into a deteriorating society would not be 100 chemists, or politicians, or professors, or engineers, but rather 100 entrepreneurs.—Abraham H. Maslow

Glaser's Law: It is easier to change a "no" to a "yes" than to change a "yes" to a "no." Agnes Allen's Law: Anything is easier to get into than to out of. Montaigne in *Essays III.x* put it this way: How far more easy it is not to enter than to get forth.

Geezer Goodies

You are financially secure when you can afford anything you want and you don't want anything.—Art Buck

Make it idiot-proof and someone will make a better idiot.—Anon

What a sober man has in his heart, a drunken man has on his lips.
—Danish proverb

Nothing impresses the mind with a deeper feeling of loneliness than to tread the silent and deserted scene of former flow and pageant.
—George Washington

Do not go where the path may lead, go instead where there is no path and leave a trail.
—Ralph Waldo Emerson

Only two things are infinite, the universe and human stupidity, and I'm not sure about the former.
—Albert Einstein

> There are more ways of killing a cat than choking her
> with cream.
> —Charles Kingsley, *Westward Ho*

Snakes, Kittens & Puppy Dogs

I have always tried to put up with snakes—because I realize that they help control the population of bugs and rodents.

Still, there are limits to my tolerance. Even rattlesnakes have an air of majesty about them . . . but like most commoners, I have never felt comfortable in the presence of royalty. For example, I refused to allow snakes to live in close proximity to my house in the country near Nashville, Tennessee.

I think it had something to do with a primordial fear of one night throwing back my bedcovers and finding a serpent sleeping there. Or, worse, NOT finding it!

One time I started to open a gate in my barn, and realized that the wooden half-door felt unusually soft along the top edge, where my hand was resting. Yes, an early-spring snake had selected that spot to stretch out and absorb the sunshine. Now, usually when the weather is a bit cool—as it was that day—snakes tend to be quite sluggish, as all cold-blooded things are. But this snake and I set new speed records, each moving rapidly in opposite directions!

I experienced snakes in the basement several times in that house, and usually used mothballs as a defense. I reasoned that since serpents rely on their sense of smell—activated by that tongue that is continually darting—maybe the smelly mothballs would disorient them and cause a migration to other places. I don't know whether it really worked—maybe the mothballs drove off the snakes' food supply of insects—but the snakes did leave when I tried it. But perhaps they were no more comfortable staying there with me around than I was with them.

Several years ago, I reprinted in my newspaper column the following account of a snake encounter that I'd found in the Petersburg, Illinois, *Observer*, written by Hattie Hamblin:

"One country gal was calling on another. Just as she drove in the lane, a big snake with a hump just a ways behind his jaws slithered out onto the white rock drive. Like most women, seeing a snake set off her internal alarm. She knew by looking at the hump, the icky creature had just lunched on an unfortunate victim.

"'I'll fix you,' she cried and stepped on the gas.

"To her delight, the force of the tires caused the snake to urp his lunch, making one live frog very, very happy.

"Overjoyed that she had saved the frog, she decided to have revenge and finish the snake off for sure. After all, what good did it do to save the frog from being the snake's lunch if he turned right around and ate it again for supper?

"She put the car in reverse, gave it the gas, and smashed—would you believe—the frog flat, making him undesirable for anyone's dinner."

The article didn't mention what happened to the snake, but my guess is that it immediately departed the location—which is what most snakes will do in similar situations. I did have one snake coil and strike at my sickle mower once. So I backed up and took another run at it. The snake, you might say, went to pieces.

I should note that this snake/frog story was reprinted in a column I wrote in 1972 and was one of very few things I've written that my mother had clipped and saved. It was returned to me when my mother passed away on March 1, 1995, at the age of 96. The snake story was followed in my column by this:

To wind up this report from the zoo, here's a "dog story," reprinted from a Kansas newspaper columnist:

"If you have children . . .

"If they've had pets . . .

"And if you live on a busy street or road, probably this has happened to you.

"Your child's pet was killed by a passing car or truck.

"It happened to our 7-year-old's pet kitten just a few days ago, for the first time, and I hope it won't happen again for a good long time to come.

"She'd had the kitten since it was born—it began its life one Sunday in a choice living room location a few minutes before we were expecting guests, no less.

"And, since she's an only child, she'd come to love the little gray kitten as a lonesome child will. Though, to be frank about it, I myself found little about the animal to love. It had an annoying habit, for one thing, of snagging its tiny—but sharp—claws on my bare feet while I had them propped on the footstool.

"The kitten was out in the front yard—my daughter later said tearfully that she had let it out herself—the morning it happened. The kitten crossed the road, saw the neighbors' dog, and started back home again just as a car was approaching. And the kitten didn't make it.

"The kitten's mistress was, as you can guess, heartbroken. To help assuage the grief, she was allowed to go a few doors up the road to play with some neighboring children.

"To them she told her sad story. They offered her a puppy in its place. I was against it, but who can hold out long in the face of a longing look like the one I saw?

"So at our home this week is a very young half-Beagle pup.

"And, when he ventures outside, he wears a collar around his neck, to which is attached a leash, to which is attached a 7-year-old girl.

"It happens that I know the people in that article. The little girl is my daughter, now married. I was the columnist who wrote it."

The half-Beagle, I think, may be the same dog that later followed us to church one morning without our knowledge—until it began howling from under a pew when the choir began singing.

With the help of a couple of other men, I managed to capture the dog and get it outside. I'll admit I was tempted for a few moments to deny knowledge of the canine's ownership before finally admitting it was mine and taking him back home and locking the dog securely in the back porch.

Geezer Gold

The follies which a man regrets most are those which he didn't commit when he had the opportunity.—Helen Rowland

There is no security on this earth; there is only opportunity.—Douglas MacArthur.

Two men look out through the same bars;
One sees the mud, and one the stars.
—Frederick Langbridge

An optimist sees an opportunity in every calamity; a pessimist sees a calamity in every opportunity.—Winston Churchill

Only she who attempts the absurd can achieve the impossible.—Sharon Schuster

> If you pick up a starving dog and make him prosperous, he will not bite you. That is the principal difference between a man and a dog.
> —Mark Twain

On My Own with a Wife, a Child, and a St. Bernard

Twice in my younger life, I lived and worked in Manhattan, Kansas, but I doubt if I'll ever be up to a third try. My first newspaper reporter's job was in that beautiful small college city at the confluence of the Kaw and Blue Rivers. After two or three few years, I had advanced to managing editor—but I'd also acquired a wife and then a child.

Nothing like getting married and having children to sharpen your focus on the future! For me, it was becoming evident that I wanted to eventually own my own publication. And, so anxious was I to acquire some skills of the printing trade that I volunteered to work free (as I'd done in high school) for a small weekly paper in a nearby town.

At my full-time job, while picking up news releases at the college's public relations office, I would always scan the bulletin board in the school of journalism to see what job offers had been posted for graduating seniors. I saw one—in Phillipsburg, Kansas, a county seat town not far from the Nebraska and Colorado borders—that appealed to me.

I mentioned it to the college's Public Relations manager, and he told me that the job was made to order for me! He said the publisher had a practice of hiring sharp young journalists, working them for a few years so they could learn the business from every angle, and then loaning them the money to buy their own newspaper.

Well, I got the job. And we moved to Phillipsburg with everything we owned in our small 1936 Ford Coupe—and found the editor had rented us a house—an unfurnished house—that he was quite proud of having arranged although I'd asked him to find us a furnished apartment. We bought a bed that day—on the installment plan—and gradually acquired other pieces, some new, some not.

I did learn the newspaper business from one end to the other at the Phillips County Review—typesetting the old Linotype way, making up ads, assembling pages, handfeeding the press or folding machine, running the contraption that imprinted a subscriber's name and address on each paper, etc. Not to mention news reporting, photography (including developing and printing, and later, making photo engravings), and selling ads and dealing with commercial printing orders.

For over a year, while my boss was secretary to the governor (he later ran for the top job himself, but didn't make it), I was the editor with full responsibility for everything except the bookkeeping. But finally I realized he was not going to back me in buying a paper—for one thing, I think he'd spent too much money pursuing a political career.

And so when my former employer in Manhattan called to see if I would be interested in running his newspapers, starting a third one from scratch, and also doing some writing for a magazine he'd started for soil conservation contractors . . . I jumped at his offer. Especially when he added that I'd get a share of the profits each year to apply toward my eventual ownership of the newspapers (he'd keep the magazine).

We found a nice rental house on the edge of the city, and I

planted my first garden—and how it grew in that fertile valley soil! And there was plenty of room for a female St. Bernard we'd acquired from the Kansas State College school of veterinary medicine. Someone had brought her there for treatment—and then abandoned her. I don't think we even had to pay anything—they were happy to find an owner for her.

Lisa didn't really eat all that much, but her bowel movements were notable. She really had a loving disposition, but did tend to discourage house-to-house salesmen by merely appearing inside the screen door.

And she looked great lying beside our fireplace in the winter. The bad news was that she was afraid of storms. So at the first clap of thunder, she sought refuge under the bed—which then had to be lifted up so that she could get back out.

At least once she followed our daughter Denise to school (about a block up the road) and the teacher called asking that we come and get the dog because it was scaring the other children at recess.

We drove a station wagon in those days, so Lisa would ride along behind the back seat when we went to visit relatives. I had to answer so many questions about her and how much it cost to feed her, etc., that I finally decided I should print up some small cards with this information, and hand them out to gas station attendants and others.

I really hated to give up Lisa when we moved to Illinois later to buy our first newspaper, but we did finally find a good home for her on a farm in Kansas.

Geezer Games

Every child is an artist. The problem is how to remain an artist once he grows up.—Pablo Picasso

Creative minds always have been known to survive any kind of bad training.—Anna Freud

He that will not apply new remedies must accept new evils, for time is the greatest innovator.—Francis Bacon

Creativity can solve almost any problem. The creative act, the defeat of habit by originality, overcomes everything.—George Lois

Don't f**k with my creativity.—Tompall Glaser

> They make a wilderness and call it peace.
> —Tacitus: A.D. 55 or 56-c, 120

Me and Wildlife

Funny thing happened to me one summertime Saturday morning when I was living alone on my little estate in Tennessee. Well, not funny ha ha, but the other kind.

Anyway, I had been hauling hay that I'd cut in my meadow to use as garden mulch. When I stopped at the house for my last cup of coffee of the morning, I turned on the TV to check for weather warnings (we'd had several days of intense thunderstorms, tornado watches and warnings).

Saturday morning is kids' time on TV, of course, and as I drank my coffee and read a magazine, I heard these characters on TV talking about snakes—how they can't hear but have an acute sense of smell via their tongue, how they look slimy but aren't, how you shouldn't pick one up unless you're sure it's not poisonous. Yeah, right.

Coffee downed, I clicked off the TV, and walked out the front door . . .

. . . and damned near stepped on a snake that was loosely coiled up right next to the doorsill. Well, I have nothing against snakes personally, but I'd learned long since that having them hang around my house definitely would cut down on my social life! This one was quite lethargic—it was still early and, anyway, the dummy was looking for warmth on the west side of the house when the morning sun was still in the east.

So I grabbed a mattock hoe that was leaning against the porch and whacked that sucker a couple of times, and then a couple more times for good measure. I swear it had a surprised look in its eyes, like . . . here I've been holding down the mouse population under your house and now you're doing this—to me?

I found partial redemption from the animal kingdom that afternoon for my act of violence. When I went to garage to get my two-wheel tractor, my friendly squirrel was about 20 feet away, searching for acorns from the big oak tree that shades the garage in summer. And, when he didn't immediately locate an acorn, the squirrel would settle instead for a maple tree seed that had fluttered that direction. We had a brief unilateral conversation— I did all the talking—but when I started the tractor motor, he scampered away.

Later that day, returning from enjoying a catfish dinner at a restaurant in town, I noted that one of my neighbors had moved several head of cows and spring calves into the pasture through which my access road runs. For the first time, I think, I noticed that all of the cows were staring at me—even the little calves stood stock still and gave me a long once over as I drove slowly among them. What were they thinking, I wondered? "There goes another one of those funny looking cows?" Maybe. Or, "Think you're big stuff, don't you . . . driving that big car when the rest of us have to walk wherever we go."

But all was not lost. When I parked the car and walked to the house, a mockingbird did its very best to tell me how great it was to be alive and well in Tennessee!

Geezer Garden

I follow nature as the surest guide, and resign myself with implicit obedience to her sacred ordinances.—Cicero

> One impulse from the vernal wood
> May teach you more of man,
> Of moral evil and of good
> Than all the sages can.
> —William Wordsworth

It is something to make two blades of grass grow where only one was growing; it is much more to have been the occasion of the planting of an oak which shall defy twenty scores of winters, or of an elm which shall canopy with its green cloud of foliage half as many generations of mortal immortalities.—Oliver Wendell Holmes.

Flowers always make people better, happier and more helpful; they are sunshine, food and medicine to the soul.—Luther *Burbank*

To travel hopefully is a better thing than to arrive—R. L. Stevenson: *El Dorado*

Geezer Guidelines

When first I thought what life should be
I described it as a comedy
For all to enjoy, for pay or free,
But then I found life was no comedy.

So then I took life seriously
Made each day count, but endlessly.
My time plod on 'till I could see
Life's not well taken seriously.

At last I learned what life must be.
And I tell you true, regretfully
That it's all a joke, yes, actually,
I know now that life is a tragedy.

A tragedy? How could it be?
After all we were taught of beauty!
And how a dream could come to be.
How then could life be a tragedy?

A child is born, but first to cry
Yet aren't tears meant to bathe the eye?
A smile's not stronger than a sigh;
And thus one by one our years go by.

We know the truth, we know we're free
To make of life what we want it to be.
But we trade our dreams for reality—
And that, my friend, is the tragedy.

LESSONS TAUGHT BY NATURE

> When Nature has work to be done,
> she creates a genius to do it.

Ralph Waldo Emerson, *Method of Nature*

Geezer Gleanings

There is a tide in the affairs of men, which, taken at the flood, leads on to fortune; Omitted, all the voyage of their life Is bound in shallows and in miseries.—Shakespeare

For of all sad words of tongue or pen, the saddest are these: "It might have been."—John Greenleaf Whittier

The worst thing one can do is not to try, to be aware of what one wants and not give in to it, to spend years in silent hurt wondering if something could have materialized—and never knowing.—David S. Viscott

To grasp the real meaning of happiness, we must think toward it with utmost clarity. Start by seeing that happiness is not the presence of an exciting feeling, but the absence of a painful feeling. When you feel no mental pain—conscious or unconscious—you are happy. In other words, true happiness is not the opposite of pain, but the absence of pain.—Vernon Howard: *The Power of Your Supermind*

"It is not a single idea, but many ideas and attitudes, including a reverence for nature and a preference for country life; a desire for maximum personal self-reliance and creative leisure; a concern for family nurture and community cohesion; a certain hostility toward luxury; a belief that the primary reward of work should be well-being rather than money; a certain nostalgia for the supposed simplicities of the past and an anxiety about the technological and bureaucratic complexities of the present and the future; and a taste for the plain and functional...."
—Editorial Credo of J. D. Belanger in *Countryside* magazine, in which the following was published in Summer 1993.

Why I Moved to the Country

J.D. Belanger's statement (quoted above) is perhaps an adequate representation of the rational side of country living for a good many, if not most, of its adherents. But I would add a quotation representative of the emotional side of the lifestyle coin, from Thoreau's *Walden II*:

"I went to the woods because I wished to live deliberately, to front only the essential facts of life, and see if I could not learn what it had to teach, and not, when I came to die, discover that I had not lived."

Or, in Robert Lewis Stevenson's words: "To be what we are,

and to become what we are capable of becoming, is the only end of life."—*Familiar Studies of Men and Books*

Although born and raised in the country, I lived my life in hopes that I might one day "return" to the farm. For in truth, though I literally was born in the country on the same bed on which I had been conceived, I was only *from* the country, and not *of* the country. As the youngest of five sons, I was excluded from most of the growing-up opportunities to learn about tractors, fence building, and animal husbandry.

Thus denied, unwittingly I am sure, my deep need to achieve early manhood, I was led at my 17th birthday to seek enlistment in the Coast Guard—a course happily endorsed by the those responsible for my high school education. Happily for me too, although they considered me a bad influence on my fellow students due to my generally rebellious attitude at the time.

"The Good Old Days?" Not for me was my purchase of a small farm in Cannon County, Tennessee, an attempt to return to those yesteryears. Growing up at the trailing edge of the Great Depression and reaching adult manhood during the dissolute decline of the World War II era, I had many reasons to look always forward to the future throughout my life, and very little inclination to turn back to seek restoration of life experiences that were representative of what I considered the worst days of my life.

I do not know for certain when the idea of living in the country first took hold of my psyche and became my destiny. Most probably it was during the declining days of my futile first marriage that resulted in termination of my greatest economic achievement: owner-publisher of a group of eight community newspapers in Illinois. Perhaps the farm's initial appeal was that of a refuge, a shelter, an asylum, a haven of security from the physical, emotional, spiritual deep well into which I had led myself.

Like most journeys to worthwhile destinations, my road to my rural retreat seems in retrospect to have led mostly uphill, continuing most of two decades. After getting out of my marriage and its associated economic entanglements, I moved to Nashville and spent the first ten years there in various music business-related enterprises, and the second decade as an advertising writer. Along the way, I first acquired two more wives—each since divorced also—and started making payments on an abandoned 55-acre woodland pasture near Nashville.

I managed to unwittingly put the cart before horse when I was divorced for the second time by first buying a Nashville condo, then selling my land at a small profit and purchasing my home for the next ten years, a two-bedroom house and acreage in Rogers Holler, just over 50 miles from Nashville. At first I continued living in the condo and spent only my weekends in the country, then lived there full time from 1989 to 1998. After renting the condo to various tenants, I accepted the fact that I was not meant to be a landlord, and sold it.

But I have begged the "why" question. What do I think is so great about living in the country? I can offer several reasons:

People. I didn't move to my farm to get away from everyone—just away from the kind of people I didn't want to be around all the time. My newspapers had surrounded a metropolitan area, but most were located in rural communities. I found that I liked the country people better than the town people. For one thing, farmers operate more out of need; less out of greed. And that is a difference that goes clear through to the soul.

Individuality. Everything I had done previously had to be accomplished through other people. Yes, most of the time I was the "boss," but was I? To succeed in business, you must put the welfare of your customers and of your employees ahead of your own wishes. And there are others you must answer to: bankers, tax collectors, the legal system, to name a few examples. But now, because I had planned for an outside income, I could practice true self-reliance.

Health. It is my well-researched opinion that humans thrive best when they eat food that is grown primarily where they live. That is, I am convinced that fruit, vegetables—even meat (though I prefer fish and foul)—that have lived in the same atmosphere that I breathe and that have gained nourishment from the same soil that I walked on are more likely to better provide me with all of the nutrients my body needs to keep me healthy and happy. So I had a large garden and grew much of my own vegetables, fruit and berries. I added fish (in two ponds that I had built) and always intended to raise poultry . . . and maybe beef.

Longevity. My mother, who died at 96, didn't begin to lose her health until she moved off the land. In my own case, I believe that having something to look forward to is essential for the mature person. Even if I were not interested in the future, nature constantly reminds me of what is to come. Thus I had to prepare the ground for planting long before I could enjoy fresh tomatoes. I needed to fence the pasture before I could raise cattle. I learned to cut wood to provide my next winter's heat source. I could seldom seek my night's rest before I had given thought to my tomorrow's activities. Thus what would happen tomorrow was always closer to my thoughts than what occurred yesterday.

Learning. Nature is our best teacher. And her school is always in session. In my "writing room" is a quotation attributed to Phaedrus, who lived in 8 A.D. "All art," he said, "is but an imitation of nature." To that I would add: "And all lessons are best learned at nature's knee." Nature teaches me about color: its hues and harmony. She teaches me about life: the beauty of a hawk circling in the wind is balanced by the violence of the kill when a prey is found. Nature teaches me about love: how the wind can at once caress then suddenly destroy; how the mighty oak and trifling dandelion struggle equally to propagate and reproduce. And nature teaches me justice: both righteous and dispassionate.

Beauty. Many metaphors defining beauty originate with nature's growing things: graceful, pleasing to the eye, attractive, dainty, gorgeous. Ask any country dweller to define beauty: As pretty as falling snow . . . as a newborn lamb . . . as a summer sunset . . . as the flowers of springtime . . . as a pretty as a picture—a picture of what? A landscape, of course.

Not live in the country? To me, it indeed would be "not living!"

* * *

I was living in Tennessee when I wrote this, but I still feel very much the same way, I suppose. Except on days like this one, when it is raining and it is chilly and there's no one here with me to provide the kind of warmth that has nothing to do with the ambient temperature!

Geezer Guidelines

The highest form of courage is the courage to create.—Rollo May

Some men see things as they are and say, "why?" I dream things that never were and say "why not?"—George Bernard Shaw (Quoted at the funeral of Bobby Kennedy by his brother, Teddy.)

It's too bad that "thinking" is not a required course in public schools. Not "remembering" but thinking I, II, III, IV.—Earl Nightingale

"My country, right or wrong" is like saying, "My mother, drunk or sober."—G. K. Chesterton: *The Defendant*

> It is something to make two blades of grass grow where only one was growing; it is much more to have been the occasion of the planting of an oak which shall defy twenty scores of winters, or of an elm which shall canopy with its green cloud of foliage half as many generations of mortal immortalities.
> —Oliver Wendell Holmes

The Nature of Nature

Some might call it a farm; others would say it was a ranch or a forest. To me, I just say that I was born in the country; farm, ranch, forest, mountains—what does it matter? I left the country at age 17, anxious to see what else the world might hold in store for me. About 40 years later, after some years of effort, I was able to return once more. And here I have stayed, in one location or another: But here, in the country.

For in my mature years, I returned—not to the same land; not even to the same part of the country. And, for some years, not even in the same country, or indeed, continent. Born in Nebraska on the southern and eastern edge of the Sandhills, raised where hay was as big and as important a crop as corn and grain, I first found when I retired my own piece of the land in Middle Tennessee. Some things were different from Nebraska. More trees, higher hills, and rocks. More rain, more humidity, less snow and cold. Still, it was the country, and the things that were the same were more in number than the features that were different.

What I really returned to was nature. And nature is the same grand lady all around this planet. Like her people, she may dress in different costumes and speak in a variety of languages. Yet, by and large, every mode of clothing has its similarities, just as nearly every language surely has words for "tree" and "grass" and "flower."

And so I was home. And home is home is home.

But before I leave my references to Nebraska and Tennessee, I must tell you a little story. Small it is in importance, larger perhaps in meaning.

Only a quarter-section of my family's home place remains, and it has been purchased by a family corporation organized by the sons and daughters of my then-oldest living brother, most of whom still reside in the state and some of whom have occupied places of respect and honor in its government. Though none live nearby, all had such good memories of a childhood of walking the pastures and meadows and splashing in the creeks that they wanted to keep ownership of those 90 acres, and so they purchased from each of us siblings our minority interest in our inheritance.

But even before the sale became a fact, they joined to repair the old farmhouse, clean up the yard of fallen trees and abandoned machinery, and to take other necessary steps to restore the fertility and productivity of the land. Those of us in the extended family are welcome to visit any time, and to use the house, and to plant and dedicate a tree to our memory if we wish.

It is an idea that deserves to be emulated by other former farm families who no longer can or want to continue operating the old family farm. As much as preservation could mean to this generation, so much more it will mean to generations yet unborn. And the land itself, cropland or otherwise, need not go out of production. For in every community there is someone who will willingly rent the otherwise unused portions for cash or on shares.

But back to my story.

A few years ago, I made one of my mostly biannual visits to

Nebraska. Wanting to bring back some of that pure Nebraska sand to loosen the tight clay soil in my garden for a carrot patch, I took along a two-bushel galvanized tub I'd picked up at an auction sale for a couple of dollars. Since I was driving a pick up then, I filled the tub with flat rocks of the kind that abounded on my land and tied it down so that it would add ballast to the otherwise unloaded pick up box. Arriving in Nebraska, I unloaded the rocks, which I imagined could be used as stepping stones to supplement the short sidewalk, and refilled the tub with sand.

Later I imagined the consternation of some 25th century geologist who might discover the Tennessee rocks in Nebraska and devote the balance of his or her career to trying to develop a theory for the geological event that caused the artifacts to have been transported halfway across the continent.

One difference between nature and man: nature does not play jokes. Nor endure for long those who would make her the butt of their pranks or jests. Many times, in fact, nature strongly resists our pitiful attempts to meddle.

For example, there was a tree filled with sharp stickers that popped up at random in my Tennessee pastures and meadow. If I let the thing grow, it flourished and spread, making it difficult to get close enough to cut it down. So, of course, (I almost said "naturally") I preferred to kill the trees out when they are mere weed size. Trouble is, when you clip it off, it comes back with a vengeance—this time popping up in four or five places in the same vicinity as if to imply that I would have been better off with one plant instead of several.

Then there's the famous or infamous Johnson grass. As the story goes, it was brought back to the southern states by a Colonel Johnson who served in Central America. In full flower, it resembles a dwarfed version of sorghum cane or related plants. Livestock treat it like grass, and it has the added virtue of making several crops a year. The down side is that it grows so profusely that other varieties are soon eliminated, and if you then try to get rid of Colonel Johnson's grass, you discover that it multiplies both above and below the ground. Yes, it makes a seed crop, and it also spreads through its rhizome roots, like crabgrass—except the roots live on through the winter. There are chemical herbicides, of course, but those of us of the organic persuasion tend to view chemicals as the nuclear bomb of agriculture.

By and large, nature will give you what you want if you can just figure out what she needs in exchange. My country home on 55 acres in Rogers Holler, Tennessee, was in splendid isolation. Except for my neighbors who lived near the top of the hill a few thousand feet away, overlooking my quiet valley.

They were good enough neighbors, but we were of two different bents. They had a good-sized family; I lived alone. They had a multitude of dogs; I had one at the most. Thus they just naturally created more sounds, drove more automobiles, had more outdoors conversations, and things like that. Since there already were a few scattered cedar trees partially blocking the view and somewhat dulling the commotion, I thought it would be a good idea to plant pine seedlings on the hillside that separates us. So I ordered 500 of them through the Soil Conservation Service from the state nursery.

And I planted them, carefully too, on 6-foot squares, reasoning that when they grew larger I could always sell or give away some of them for Christmas trees. About three years later, I had maybe two dozen of them of which a half-dozen were flourishing and the balance seemed to teeter between bare survival and total death. This despite mowing, mulching, even some watering via hand-carried buckets. I realized then that I lived in Cedar tree country. Pines were not welcome there.

About the same time, I noticed several baby Maple trees sprouting here and there each spring, so I transplanted a couple dozen of the best to fill in some of the gaps left by departed pine trees. The Maples flourished, many of them right next to anemic-looking pine seedlings.

Why? I didn't care. I just wanted to find more little Maples to transplant. Go with the winner, I always say. But obviously the soil was better suited to Maples than to Pines.

Another lesson from nature is the importance of reproduction—what we humans call sex. We usually treat sex as a means of pleasure, but nature is downright serious about it. Plants that flower do so to make seeds. Cut the flowers or even pull off the dead blossoms and what happens? More flowers. So there'll be more seeds. And of course the flowers themselves owe their color and beauty to little tricks the plants had developed over the years to aid survival and attract the insects that pollinate them. We treat sex like a forbidden subject and hide it behind closed doors. Nature does it right out in the open.

Geezer Gospel

And this our life, exempt from public haunt,
Finds tongues in trees, books in the running brooks,
Sermons in stones, and good in everything.
 —Shakespeare, *As You Like It*

Nature I have loved, and next to nature, art.—W. S. Lander

For what has made the sage or poet write
But the fair paradise of Nature's light?
 —Keats, *I Stood Tip-toe*

I have loved not man the less, but nature more.—Byron: *Childe Harold IV*

Never does nature say one thing and wisdom another.—Juvenal: *Satires XIV*

> All animals are equal, but some animals are more
> equal than others.
> George Orwell: *Animal Farm*

Nature's Law of Compensation

Compensation must be one of nature's laws.

On a Monday when I was living in the hills and hollers of Tennessee, I decided to saw up the tree that had died and blown down near the pond. And soon I had accumulated a good-sized pile of split firewood, ready to be hauled to the house and stacked outside of the basement door. Being long since dead, the wood did not require a curing period as does green wood.

Being a devoutly lazy person who doesn't mind working hard but always looks for the easy way to do it, I decided to back the pickup partway down the hill so I wouldn't have to carry the wood all the way to the top of the hill. I recognized some possible danger in this, because the hill is fairly steep. But I reasoned that with a few hundred pounds of wood in the box, I'd have no trouble getting back up the hill.

As it turned out, a big rock hidden in the grass made it difficult to first get down the hill, and then, of course, that much more difficult to get back up. Just as I realized that I was for sure hung up on the rock and thus in trouble, I turned off the truck engine just in time to hear a tractor on the road up the hill from my hollow (or holler, as we say). But too late, the tractor was outward bound and was long gone in a matter of a couple of minutes.

Anyway, I rather enjoy these challenges. I always said that I was not trying to be self sufficient—people do need people, sometimes. But I was trying to be self reliant. Whatever needs to be done, I think I should be able to use my back and brain to cause it to happen. Sounds good, but at the time you actually face the problem, it doesn't really feel all that good.

So I needed a plan. First thing, I fetched my "come-along," a hand lever-powered hoisting apparatus. I knew I couldn't drag that truck up the hill with it, but maybe if I tried it would suggest something else to try. And I quickly discovered that I could in fact move the truck an inch or two. And, additionally, when I tried moving the truck under its own power, the hoist at least kept the truck from sliding farther back down the hill.

But first, I had to deal with the fact that I had nothing very substantial to hook it onto. The attached cable wasn't long enough to reach the barn, and I didn't have a chain or another cable. Although, I remembered that when I attended a farm sale two or three weeks ago, the log chains were all that I had bid on, albeit unsuccessfully.

So, at first I tried driving a steel post in the ground, and pulling against it . . . but of course this didn't work too well and, besides, the post wasn't portable, and I'd have to reset it each time I moved the truck a few more inches closer to the hilltop. So, since my own tractor was broke down, I would have to start the "spare" car and use it for an anchor. The battery was down, and coasting it down a small incline didn't build up enough speed to start the motor. So I hooked up the battery charger, and waited. And, waiting, I gazed idly toward my pond.

Suddenly, a big, ungainly looking water bird of some kind swooped in and landed about two feet away from the water's edge!

"Hey!" I yelled, probably because I immediately realized I was looking at the reason there weren't many fish in my pond. The bird, who apparently hadn't even noticed me, took off and flew a few feet above the ground across the pasture and down to my other pond. Well, if it was eating my fish it probably also was responsible for decreasing the frog population from the thousands of tadpoles I'd seen last spring to a dozen or two full-grown leapers who currently seemed to be in residence.

Then I heard dogs barking, and looked toward the sound and saw two deer—a buck and a doe—loping leisurely along with hardly a backward glance at three of my neighbor's dogs that were pursuing them, and losing ground with every yelp. It was a beautiful scene. And though it lasted only a few seconds because the deer soon entered the woods and outdistanced the dogs completely, it is a picture that has remained in my memory since that day.

By then, the battery was recharged enough to start the car. I drove it into position, locked the brakes, turned the ignition off, and put it in low gear, then attached the come-along. And next, inch by inch, I used the pickup's 2WD power to move the truck forward a couple inches, then take up the slack with the hoist, then repeat the sequence. It got the job done, and within an hour of my initial difficulty, the truck was back up the hill, the car's battery was well charged up, and I was enjoying recalling the two treats that nature had offered me that day.

A couple of days later, it was raining and so I found it to my advantage to spend the day working inside of the house. About midafternoon, I decided I needed to take a walk or something, and as I stepped outside the back door, I heard the sound of several dogs raising a ruckus in my front yard. Coming around the corner of the house, I saw the reason.

Three of my neighbor's hounds had treed one small, very scared squirrel in the red maple tree. The squirrel was out at the end of a small branch, looking desperately for a tree close enough to leap into. Of course, the little bushy-tailed fellow could have just waited it out in the tree he already was in . . . but then I don't suppose every squirrel is born knowing that most dogs can not climb trees. So the squirrel made a suicide leap toward the next tree and fell to the ground, but landed will all four legs and his tail pumping away for dear life, literally.

He almost made it. The three hounds were frozen in canine astonishment for a second or two, and the squirrel was halfway to a big oak tree by the time the dogs figured out what was happening. But halfway was no way, and the squirrel met his doom within seconds. In fact, the entire episode probably didn't take five seconds to play out.

Like I said, nature usually offers compensations. Trouble is, sometimes she just doesn't know when to stop.

Geezer Games
RATE SCHEDULE

Answers to Questions $1.00

Answers Which Require Thought 10.00

Correct Answers 15.00

Looks of Total Noncomprehension FREE

> I have often thought that if heaven had given me choice of my position and calling, it should have been on a rich spot of earth, well watered, and near a good market for the productions of the garden. No occupation is so delightful to me as the culture of the earth, and no culture comparable to that of the garden.
>
> Thomas Jefferson, written in 1811 after serving as our third president

Gardening on the Right Side of the Brain

Yes, you can have your own green thumb... you can enjoy gardening without making complicated plans, without keeping year-to-year detailed records, or without research to learn what experts advise every time you pick up a hoe, rake, or shovel.

I think of it as "gardening on the right side of the brain," based on the title of a guide for artists, *Drawing on the Right Side of the Brain*. In that book, author Betty Edwards points out—as others have—that the two sides of the brain control different functions. The right side is more involved with our emotions, our creativity, our subconscious mind. The left side, on the other hand, is the more orderly, mathematical, cognitive part of the brain.

If you love to cook, maybe you use a right-brain creative approach. That is, perhaps you like to "enhance" a recipe...

add your own touch. Or come up with a substitute when you lack one or more ingredients. Maybe invent your own dishes without even opening a cook book. If so, you are a creative cook!

On the other hand, the left-brain method would be to slavishly follow every recipe word for word, cup for cup, teaspoon by teaspoon. And if you're out of pecans but do have a supply of shelled walnuts—well, you either find another recipe or take time for a trip to the store to buy more pecans.

The true right-brain chef takes a quick look at the larder and refrigerator, then concocts a recipe on the spot, using what's on hand, adding this or that spice or herb to create a taste that is different, perhaps, but good.

Right-brained gardeners don't concern themselves too much if the weather is too cold or too wet the day they have available to plant peas. Instead, they plant 'em as soon as they can, but figure out their own methods of helping the delayed seeds make up for lost time—extra organic feeding, perhaps. Or aluminum foil reflectors to enhance the sunlight and help the late-started plants catch up.

"Creative thinking" does not limit itself to designing a new "look" for your garden or trying new hybrids. And it is more than deciding that you are not restricted in discovering new ways to harvest, preserve, or serve the produce derived from your labors.

Rather, creative thinking is a way of approaching "problems" by using a new combination of things you already know. It is a method of drawing upon your subconscious—by using the right side of your brain—for help in reassembling the various components of your knowledge into one new complete package of "solutions."

And keep in mind that I use the word "problem" advisedly. Most people connect "problem" to "worry" but that's not necessarily true. More simply stated, for our purpose a "problem" is anything that can be altered by a "solution." Many times, of course, you may even discover the solution long before anyone recognized the problem!

Creative thinking involves a six-step process—and this same process will work for you in the garden, in the kitchen, with your family, or in your job.

1. Develop the creative attitude. In other words, you can't find anything if you don't look for it. And you won't look unless you make a habit of looking. For example, look out a window. Be aware of what you see when you look. Now consider how you would be more aware of seeing every detail if instead you looked at a photograph taken from that same window. Everything that you would see in the photo could have been seen with the naked eye . . . but you weren't looking for everything, so you didn't look at everything. Individually, we tend to focus on one thing at a time. The camera, on the other hand, records all within sight of its lens. You can develop your creative attitude by making a habit of seeing things you aren't looking for, or don't expect to see.

2. Define and analyze the problem. What's your goal? Three crops of beans a year in the same rows? Less backbreaking work in the garden and bigger harvests? But be careful! Sometimes the real goal likes to hide inside of the surface definition of the problem. It's something like a medical doctor's need to know whether he's dealing with a symptom or a disease. Personally, I find I'm more likely to solve a problem that I have trouble defining if I reverse the effort and try instead to simplify the problem by giving it a one-word or two-word name.

For example:

We must not be planting enough cabbage because we run out long before spring. Or maybe we're eating too much cabbage because we don't grow enough similar crops—broccoli, Brussels sprouts, etc. Or could it be that we plant plenty of cabbage but harvest it too soon, or lose too many heads to insects, or something else?

So you could do a lot of research in an attempt to define and analyze. Or you could oversimplify: More Cabbage. Either way you have defined a problem and, even taking the simplified route, you have also provided analysis: our family needs more cabbage.

3. Seek out and fill your mind with facts. If you're like me, you probably can go easy on the "seek out" part. You read gardening publications. You have a few garden books on your library shelves. You talk gardening now and then. And maybe you watch a gardening show on public television. Plus, you pay attention to what you read in seed catalogs and the like.

Chances there a lot of "facts" already are stored in your mind's data base. But if you're in doubt, it won't hurt to do a little more research and some additional reading on the subject. Might help you remember what you already know!

4. Make note of any ideas for a solution that pop into your head, no matter how "off the wall" they seem. Now, if you're serious about this, you'll write each idea down as it occurs to you. With some practice, likely you'll develop an ability to make a mental note of these ideas as they occur to you. Main thing is, don't make the mistake of thinking that the first solution you think of is the only one, or the best one. Many times, of course, the first idea is the best—but not always. Give your subconscious a chance to make more than one or two suggestions on the subject. Doesn't hurt to engage in some "interior debate" so long as you don't fall into the trap of looking for the *only* "rational" or "right" answer.

Another tip: Think of the solution when you're on the scene of the problem. How far apart to plant the apple trees? Go walk around in your orchard area. Ideas come easier when you are on location, so to speak.

5. This is the easy one. Time now to relax and let it all simmer in your subconscious mind. I remember reading once that Joseph Wambaugh, the Los Angeles cop turned novelist, often was criticized by his wife for hanging around the swimming pool. "But honey," he'd protest, "I'm working!" After his first couple of

runaway bestsellers, the argument was ended. To make up things out of your head, whatever works, works.

Personally, the best way for me to relax is through mild physical activity. I've never been a "workout addict" or distance runner. To me that kind of exercise is as wasteful as those all-to-frequent "walks for humanity" when participants seek pledges based on how many miles they will walk. How is humanity helped? Well, from the money raised, say sponsors of these events. But how does the walking help to "earn" the money? It draws attention to the need, say participants.

I have an alternative suggestion: How about a "Clean up the parks for humanity day"? I'd donate much quicker if the "walker" spent the same time and energy cleaning up a city park, or picking up trash along the highway, or plowing, planting, and tending a garden for someone too old, feeble, or handicapped to do it for themselves.

But each of us has the right to play the game of life by our own rules. So if drinking a couple of beers and watching a football game on television helps you relax, then do your thing and I'll do mine!

6. Set a day and time and make your decision. It's not totally necessary to make an appointment with yourself in advance. Quite likely you'll make your decision whenever and wherever you are ready to make it. Main thing is, don't just let it drag on. If you haven't "felt" the answer deep down to your toes, then maybe you need to prompt your creative side—your right brain—by telling yourself something like "today at 1 p.m. I'm going to take another look at my garden and decide what to plant after I dig up the potatoes." Then follow through. At 1 p.m., stand next to the potatoes and the answer to your question will appear. Not written in the sky, nor spelled out in clay clods on the ground. But the answer will be there for you—in your conscious mind.

I want to warn you, however. Sometimes the subconscious mind can play little tricks on you.

A few years ago, I actively began practicing a method of

communication with the subconscious espoused by Joseph Murphy in his fascinating book, *The Power of Your Subconscious Mind*. Part of the procedure—some might call it prayer—is to remind myself each night as I am drifting off to sleep of five or six one-word life goals. Two of those goals I sum up in the words "Peace and Prosperity." (As a writer, I've always found alliteration appealing. Whoops, there I go again!)

One of my "conscious mind" goals came true when I bought my first farm. I was happy with the purchase, and after visiting the site a dozen times, I decided to return home by a different route. And at a crossroads just a few miles away from the farm, I came upon a sign that read: "Prosperity: 5 miles." Of course I had to go see it, and found that the "city" consisted of two churches and a cemetery! Immediately I realized that the money I was using to buy the farm came from my job as advertising copywriter for a national religious publishing company.

A couple of years passed, and I was offered a 25% profit for the land, and so I sold it—and immediately started searching for another site. Finally, I settled on one that I wanted to see—it was the right size, in the area I preferred, and priced close to my budget.

Driving me out to look at it, the real estate agent decided to take a short cut on the spur of the moment. And within two minutes we passed a church with a sign proclaiming that it was the "Prosperity Bible Church."

I decided to buy that farm. I was more than satisfied with the purchase and that made my life peaceful. And my work continued to make me prosperous too!

My other four "prayer goals?" Life, Love, Health, Happiness. You'll have to take my word for it: they have come to pass also—and my life based on creative thinking has had a lot to do it. I've mentioned this "prayer system" before, but I repeat it here—because I think it important.

> If Winter comes, can Spring be far behind?
> —Percy Bysshe Shelley: *Ode to the West Wind, V*

Spring Comes to Tennessee

Spring arrives gently in Tennessee and throughout the Mid-South. By late February and occasionally earlier, residents enjoy a four-or five-day string of "nice days" when the temperatures soar to the 60s or 70s during the day, then drop back to near freezing around the lonely 4 a.m. hour. The impatient gardener seizes the opportunity to plant potatoes and English peas, although tomatoes and melons may be more on the mind.

And in early March you can spot the greening of tree twigs at the side the road or in the woodlot. The flowering bushes lead the way, followed by flowering trees—the Bradford pear, then the Redbud, Dogwood, and others. Not all of the same variety leaf out nor bloom at once—nature is still tentative and selective, fearing like the gardener the sudden return to icy temperatures. Even within the same variety, only those bushes and trees with maximum sunlight exposure will bloom early. Others, shadowed by city building or country hillside, like to lag behind their brash brothers and sisters.

But it is the earth itself that first betrays the onset of the vernal equinox. Dandelions, wild onion, and other opportunistic but unacceptable plants green up and sometimes flower. The cool season grasses—like Kentucky Fescue—rouse at the roots and begin their twice-yearly growing sprees. Of course, there are the buttercups and the other members of a limited assortment of early flowering bulbs that are in bloom, sometimes with their finery suddenly surrounded by a late snowfall.

The days grow much, much longer as spring emerges, and the dogs spend more time hanging around the yard following their nighttime meal. In winter, the dogs gobble their food, slurp a quick drink of water, and perhaps take time for one or two other bodily functions before trotting tidily toward their warmer sleeping quarters.

Now, as the sun stays longer in the western sky, the dogs seek out their favorite observation points as remembered from last summer and peer blank-eyed into the oncoming early dusk, perhaps hoping against hope that a rabbit or other animal of choice will pop magically into view. In vain they watch, but they watch until darkness finally triumphs.

Just as we annually seek a sincere February spring, good fortune is always anticipated, sometimes remembered. But seldom repeated.

> Living systems move through disorder on a path to a new and better order as a necessary process of healthy living. Welcome disorder as a challenge. The universe is not a balance—it's a chaotic miracle. Death is the only biological equilibrium. So life must be always lacking in equilibrium.
> –Paul Pearsall: *Making Miracles*

Things You Might Learn From Nature

I have always been curious about "how things work." How do trees grow, how do birds survive, where do fish live, and so on? As I got older, I also became curious about how my life and everyone's lives "work." (One writer said that humans spend their lives preparing for something that never happens.)

So I read a lot, and thought a lot, and when I had the opportunity—which was not often—I talked and listened to people who thought about or had studied about these things. And, mostly, I wound up with more questions and found few answers.

Always I've felt a pull toward "the country," toward living on a farm again, so when the chance came, I bought my little house and 55 acres. I lived there 10 years, out where nature manifests itself slowly through trees and weeds and bugs and animals . . . lifeforms that exist as they really are and in relatively slow motion. Humans, on the other hand, seem do their best to conceal their real existence from each other, and try hard to speed up most aspects of their lives.

The temptation is strong to attempt to define exactly what I have learned from nature, and I don't know that I should or even if I could do that. So this is not a definitive list, just some random thoughts:

1. Things happen. And for most of the things that happen there is no reason, no explanation other than the ones we make up in hopes of finding some kind of order in the universe. Since whatever "order" we perceive is the product of our wishful thinking, the truth must be that the only "order" is "disorder." If it hasn't happened, it probably will—or it already has and we just didn't notice it.

2. No one, no thing is "to blame." People (like other living things) just do the things they do because that's what seemed like the right (or only) option for them at that time.

3. If other people aren't to blame for the dumb things that they do, then neither are you nor I to blame for the dumb things we might have done. Or, in my case, admittedly I did do!

4. The only difference between me and, say, a dog is that I have the ability to think consciously. Between the two of us, the dog has the advantage. For example, every time the dog and I would go near a certain brush pile, my dog suddenly remembered she once almost caught a rabbit there, and she would tear off to check out the same spot again. What she didn't remember was that she didn't catch that rabbit the first time. But that is exactly what I would remember... and why I wouldn't bother trying to do it again and again. And so I would miss a second chance of catching a rabbit because I'd remember "failure" while my dog remembered "opportunity."

5. If you assume that the dog is after all more likely to catch a rabbit by trying to find one than by reasoning as a human would that there is no use trying because of past failures, that is why humans also might make their best decisions on a SUB-conscious level. Even better if the decision is based on a generality

instead of a specific. If I were a dog, for example, I wouldn't want a rabbit; that is too specific; it narrows my chance of achievement. What I really want is food. So when I keep the image of food before my subconscious mind, it will lead me to a rabbit, squirrel, or even today's batch of dog food. No matter which; what a dog knows it needs is food.

(The dog, by the way, didn't just check her dish for food in the morning and at night—my usual feeding times. She checked every time she passed that spot. And, a few times, her persistence paid off.)

Humans vary as to how set in stone their own little routines may be. But we all have many things we do by rote; things we do or we don't do because of our rational expectations. For example, we don't check the mailbox on Sunday. But quite possibly someone other than the postal worker might (albeit illegally) put something in your mailbox for you on a Sunday or holiday.

6. The thing that scares us is often the very thing that could help us. (Nietzsche says that harm comes to us not from the strong but from the weak!) But I'm not talking so much about physical fear as about psychological fear—fear buried so deep we have to turn around real fast to even see its shadow. It is difficult to give an example of this because my own fears are so deeply repressed that my mind objects to even considering the possibility of describing them. I think you probably are acquainted with your own nemesis—if not by name then at least by reputation. Next time even a little teeny tiny fear pops up, just trample right on through it. Then you'll see what is meant by saying the thing that scares us is often the thing that could help us. Doing the thing we don't want to do is, I admit, more difficult than doing the easy thing. But the pay-off for the former is much greater. Remember, we are not talking about courage here. It's more akin to disregarding that little voice that says, no, you don't want to do that.

7. The big difference between "weeds" and "crops" (other than that a weed is a crop no one has found a profitable use for) is that weeds, left alone in life's struggle, have been forced to

adapt themselves to their growing medium, the soil. Crops, on the other hand, being forced to adapt themselves to the needs of the grower, have acquired certain specific prerequisites from their growing medium. All life is a form of energy. If a corn stalk has to use the bulk of its energy to produce a fairly uniform ear of corn, then it has little energy left to deal with variations in the soil's moisture, temperature, minerals, insects, and food content. Dandelions, on the other hand, are free to flower any old way they want to—on tall stems if because of competing plants that is what's necessary to reach the sunlight, or on very short stems if needed to escape the lawn mower's blade.

Same principle holds for humans. If we put all of our energy into "living" our life, there isn't much left over to use in thinking about it. Or vice versa. Now, I don't know which is the "right" way to live one's life—doing or thinking. But, then, neither do the dandelions nor the corn. But I do think a weed's life is similar to what ours can be if we rely more on our subconscious mind or higher self.

So that's why I suggest: Try spending some time with nature. You may like it! And I'll guarantee that if you keep your eyes open, you'll learn some things.

In his younger days a man dreams of possessing the
heart of the woman whom he loves; later, the feeling
that he possesses the heart of a woman may be enough
to make him fall in love with her.
—Marcel Proust: *Swann's Way in Remembrance of
Things Past*

Lonesome Is As Lonesome Does

It was easing up to a summer twilight when I heard the knock on my front door. An unexpected knock, since I lived a couple of miles off the Tennessee hard road, down a winding dirt and rock drive that few salesmen and only one politician ever had the guts to travel. It was a few seconds before I could locate my TV's remote control, then find the mute button, and put aside the supper I'd been eating out of the same pot in which I'd cooked it. "Gourmet cooking," I've been told, "is when you start with a spanking clean pot or pan."

"Didn't wake you up, did I?" It was a question country people in my part of Tennessee liked to pose anytime there was a delay in answering the phone or coming to the door, regardless of the time of day. I said "nope," then realized that although I'd answered his first knock, since I hadn't heard or seen his pickup truck coming in my driveway, I'd violated custom by failing to come out on the porch or walk into the yard to greet my visitors.

The middle-aged, portly, redheaded and red-bearded man massaged his whiskers gently and said, "First time I've been all the way down the road into this holler." Like I said before, I didn't get many uninvited visitors. My road, which served only four homesteads, started out from the highway like your ordinary dirt and rock road, then went over a stock gap, fashioned of widely spaced narrow wood planks that discouraged livestock from walking across them. The road got narrower and bumpier as it then wound between the vacant house and the barn of another man's farm, climbed precariously up a hill, then crossed a second stock gap before a curving descent into the little valley where my house, garage, and barn sat, half-hidden in summer by the trees. Another half-mile past my driveway, the road dead-ended in an abandoned farmyard.

Since the road earned only a minimum attention from the county road crew, and the right-of-way was often in possession of cows or goats that gave way to vehicles with great reluctance, the man who delivered the daily newspaper from the city refused my subscription. Only the postal service and the package delivery people were willing to make the trip. That was no problem for me, since it deflected most uninvited visitors.

On the other hand, the poor state of repair of the road and stock gaps tended to make me decide to just stay home on rainy days even when I was bored or on sunny Saturdays when I was in need of only a couple of things. So I usually saved up my trips to town until I lacked something important—like gas for the tractor or ice cream for me.

I still hadn't said anything beyond "nope" to the red-bearded stranger, so he turned slightly and swung a massive arm in the general direction of an unoccupied, decaying mobile home that sat a few yards from my neat farm cottage. The mobile home was unused except by the English Spaniel dog I'd adopted after his owner married a woman who already had two dogs of her own. The dog liked to sleep under the trailer because that's where she used to hang out at her previous home. Without seeming to look,

I noted that the stranger's noble beer gut also tried to turn toward the mobile home, but was forced to give up the effort about halfway of the distance.

"Your neighbor's son down the road—I forget his first name—said he bought some baled hay off you last week, and said you might want to sell that mobile home."

"Yeah, I would," I said, and to prove it, added: "I have to pay insurance on the darned thing. I moved out here to get some distance from everybody in the city, but all the time people with a carload of kids keep stopping in and wanting to rent it. So I'd just as soon sell it and be done with it."

We started walking toward the mobile home, and I saw a woman of about the right age, size, and general look to be Red's wife coming toward us from his truck. Her body was shaped like a man's from her head down, but her hair was a dead giveaway. Looked like she might have spent too much time under the dryer last time she had a permanent. Hair so tightly curled her scalp showed through.

"Like I say," I went on, "main reason I moved out here was to get away from being right up next to people, people, people all the time. So I sure don't want to bring 'em right on my property."

I guess she heard what I was saying, because by the time she reached us, her mouth was already in high gear. "How long you lived here?" she said. About a year, I replied. "How'd you happen to move out here? That's something I always ask newcomers," she said, the only time she made any effort to explain or preface one of her numerous questions or comments.

I told her I'd taken early retirement and wanted a place where I could have a big garden.

Red, meanwhile, was asking questions also, mostly about the mobile home, telling me his "missus" wanted one to open a craft shop. All the while, Mrs. Red continued to probe my personal business. How long you been in Tennessee. About 20 years. Where did you work? Nashville. For the state? No, for a publishing company. How's your wife like it out here? Don't have one at the moment, I told her.

"Well, now," she said. "I wish I could fix you up with this friend of mine. She's the sweetest thing. About 40 years old and if she's ever done anything wrong in her life, why, nobody has ever heard about it. Not like her twin sister. Not at all. That one's been married twice and all that."

During the few seconds it took Red to check out the trailer's walk-in closet, I said to Mrs. Red: "To tell you the truth, I would like to get acquainted with some ladies out here. I don't much want to start dating somebody in Nashville again. Too far to drive back and forth, and besides, they probably wouldn't want to give up their city life and move away out here."

Red was in the mobile home kitchen now, asking me if the refrigerator and stove worked. And I told him I thought they did, but I'd never had the electricity turned on in the mobile home, so I couldn't say for sure.

"Well," his wife went on. "You're too late for her. She's got cancer, poor thing. Gonna die before she ever had a chance to live."

Red and I concluded our discussion, and his wife went back to the truck, more words than I had time to hear still trailing out behind her as she walked away. Her husband and I walked over to the house to get pen and paper so we could trade phone numbers, and I apologized for the messy living room, saying something about me being a typical bachelor who only cleaned house when he was expecting company. "Shoot," said Red, "looks cleaner than our house." He went out to his truck then, and they drove away.

Me, I re-heated my supper, thinking all the while about what had been said. And finished eating.

Then I filled and lit my pipe and went back to watching the television. As usual, it wasn't nearly as interesting as real life.

> Backward, turn backward, O Time, in your flight,
> Make me a child again, just for tonight!
> —Elizabeth Akers Allen: *Rock Me to Sleep*

Life As a Lad in the 'Good Old Days'

I have been rich and I've been poor and being rich is better, goes the old saying. Well, sure it is, but I really doubt that there need be much difference so far as our inner life is concerned.

Of course, I've never been to the extreme edges of either, really. I've been out of money a time or two or twenty, even some times when I didn't have the slightest idea where the next dollar would come from. The key thing is this: you have to do something when that happens to you. Don't sit around waiting for someone to come along and rescue you. And if you go on the take (sign up for welfare, etc.) you may forfeit your self-respect, and that would be a serious loss.

This may account for the extreme pride I've noticed in down-on-their-luck people. If pride is all you have left, you are less inclined to surrender it.

For the last few years, I've been as "rich" as I've ever been, although I prefer the word "prosperous." To me, prosperity means

I have the money to buy most anything I might need—new clothes or a new car. But I try to live my life a lot like I did just a few years ago when I perforce managed to exist on $10 worth of groceries a week.

Spending money makes some people feel better, just like eating tends to make us feel better. But just as eating all the time makes you feel worse sooner or later, so does overspending or shopping for things you don't need. Both habits eventually can cause you more harm than good.

When I do get the urge to shop without reason, I head for a secondhand store. I can spend a couple of hours there, and make a lot of purchases (things I really think I need too!) and maybe pay $5 or $10. A couple of hours in a big shopping mall would cost me $50 or $100, and much of the stuff I'd tote home wouldn't make my life any better than the secondhand stuff would.

Because I grew up during the 'thirties, experiencing the twin devils of drouth and depression, there was never much cash money around our house. Or around any house, for that matter. The county superintendent of schools, I remember hearing then, earned the princely sum of $100 a month! That seemed like more money than anyone could possibly need.

Our big entertainment opportunity each week came on Wednesday nights, when the Carlin Theatre in Spalding, Nebraska, would hold "Family Night." Parents and children were admitted for 25 cents per family. And Mr. Carlin would look the other way if you brought along a cousin or two.

Our best chance of "getting to go to the show" was when some piece of farm machinery had broken down that day and my dad needed to buy a new part (the stores stayed open long enough for country folk to do their "trading" before the movie began). Second best chance was if it looked like rain—or had already rained enough to keep us out of the fields the next day. My mother seldom went to the movies with us on Wednesday night . . . I suspect she was happy to get us all out of the house for a couple of hours.

Visiting relatives was another form of entertainment, though I never looked at it that way. Usually it meant Sunday dinner after church. Evening visits took place mostly in the wintertime, and were often either a card party or a dance. If the latter, my father would be advised to bring his "fiddle" along. Occasionally people would visit on a Sunday afternoon (after "dinner" unless the visit was prearranged), sometimes stopping at more than one home per Sunday.

County fair time (we'd go to both the Wheeler and Greeley County Fairs) brought the big events of the year. When I was old enough to have a 4-H Club calf, I once got to stay at the fairgrounds all night. Otherwise, we'd attend at least two days and two evenings. Wheeler County (Bartlett) was centered around a rodeo, with a raucous beer-drinking dance each evening.

Greeley County (Spalding) was into baseball, and managed to import some type of grandstand entertainment for one night. That's where I saw and heard my first electric organ. Spalding also had a dance, but it was outdoors and well lighted—no place for the drinkers to sneak off for a snort, thus much more decorous than the Bartlett events. And not nearly as much fun!

When I'm watching television, or listening to my stereo, I remember how simple our pleasures were in my youth. And how much we would have appreciated television then! But we did enjoy radio—probably more than we enjoy TV today. For one thing, the quality of programming seemed better. Maybe that was because we didn't expect so much, or maybe it was because radio left much more to the imagination.

Anyway, I understand why today's "poverty" people need a TV set. When you don't have any money, you have a lot of time. And maybe vice versa?

My oldest brother was a radio freak, and when my dad brought home our first radio, they often used the batteries from the telephone for the radio. In later years, my brother hooked up a loudspeaker system to the telephone so that we could eavesdrop on the "party line" without even picking up the phone receiver.

And I hit the pits of despair the time I blew out a tube on our only radio in the dead of winter when we were snowed in and couldn't get to town to buy a new tube. Worst of it was that I did it by idly and unthinkingly touching a loose wire to a part of the radio. It was a dumb thing to do, and as a result we had no radio to listen to for several days—and nothing new to read either, since the mail was not being delivered because of the storm. And that was all the punishment I needed!

Geezer Gold

Why do some people talk one way but sing another? (e.g.: Cindi Lauper, ABBA, or the Beatles) *Atlantic* magazine's March 1991 issue explained: "The space above the voice box, the supraglottal cavity, tends to assume a different shape during singing (as compared, I suppose, to its shape when talking).

"The supraglottal configuration is responsible for the way we pronounce vowels, and vowel sounds are very important in the production of an accent. During singing the supraglottal configuration is highly consistent among singers of any particular type of music (whether it is pop, blues, or opera). In regular speech, however, the configuration of their supraglottal cavities may vary widely."

I've also been told that we're born with the ability to sing, but some of us can't carry a tune or strike a true note because of our conditioning. Hey, something else to blame on your parents.

> We triumph without glory when we conquer without danger.
> —Corneille: *Le Cid*

Me and My Chainsaw

When I moved to my farm and decided to use the existing Ashley heater and burn wood, I didn't know a whole heck of a lot about cutting down trees and sawing up the logs. Not from hands-on experience, anyway. Because, you see, I grew up in the Sandhills of Nebraska and trees there were prized highly. When the first settlers arrived in Nebraska, trees were so scarce the homesteaders had to build their houses out of sod, and burned twists of hay and buffalo chips for heat to cook food and keep warm in the winter. In case you didn't know, "buffalo chips" are dried manure piles.

Of course, Nebraska has lots of trees now. J. Sterling Morton, who founded Arbor Day, was a native of Nebraska City (just off the interstate south of Omaha), and if you ever pass that way, his home is worth a visit.

Of course, there already were quite a few trees around by the time I was born, but not so many that we would cut one down just for wood to burn in the stove. Those destroyed by wind we sawed up and burned, yes. But not using a chainsaw. Instead, with a big belt-driven whirling blade attached to the front of the tractor. And we also burned lots and lots of corncobs (though corncobs were reputed to have another use, we used old Sears catalogs for that).

So, when I figured out that my acres were about half woodland, I also realized that some day, somehow, I would have to learn how to use a chain saw. And I did. But it took a while.

The first year, when I still lived in the city and only spent weekends on my land, I used a hand bow saw and an axe to cut the small amount of firewood I needed. Slow it was, but the extra exercise was an added benefit; I'm sure I got a week's worth of workout over each two-day weekend.

By the second year, I'd invested in an electric powered chainsaw. I would use muscle power to cut the trees down and into manageable lengths, then haul the logs back to the house and there slice them into stove-long size. Is the electric-powered saw safer than the gasoline model? Yes, I think it is. For one thing, it stops quicker. And it doesn't go as fast.

But maybe the biggest safety factor comes from the fact that the electric saw always starts. That's right. It always runs. There is no temperamental rope-cranked engine that sometimes refuses to do right and get on with it. So there's not the same chance that the operator will be so ticked off by the time he gets the saw running that he forgets what he is doing and winds up hurting himself.

I'll tell you what made me so safety conscious. Long before I even thought about using a chainsaw myself, I read in the Nashville newspaper about some guy in a neighboring county who had sawed off some important male body parts, and how the surgeons had worked tirelessly for hours on his behalf, trying to stitch him and his manhood back together. One doesn't forget something like that easily! That story really made an impression on me, and will stay alive in my memory long after the phone numbers of former woman friends are forgotten.

So I always tried to be careful. One trick I used a lot was not to take the gas and oil mixture with me. Within an hour, the tank would run dry, and I would have to stop and walk back to the house for more. That was just the break I needed, for otherwise after an hour or so I became so accustomed to cutting down trees and sawing them up that the work became automatic. And I was not ready yet to turn over the job of handling a wicked tool like a chainsaw to my subconscious mind.

The trees on my land hadn't been taken care of much, and so for the first few years I worked mostly on the dead trees, and thinning out the stands, and so on. But since I have a low threshold for boredom, I tried to include as much variety as possible.

For example, I would work in four or five different spots, so I didn't have to go back to the same place over and over. I tried to set one target goal each season, and do everything that needed to be done in one area—cutting, thinning, clearing low limbs and weeds or brush, and replanting, if necessary. But I also did other things in other places as I cut wood—opening up a road here, cutting trees to leave a walking path at another site, cutting out junk trees to reclaim pasture land still elsewhere.

Sure, I know, you're saying that's a great way to work when you don't have to earn a living. And you are right. When I worked to earn a living, I did what had to be done when it needed to be done. And, I might say shyly, I did a damned good job of it. Part of the reason I worked so hard then was so I could do only what I really wanted to do when the day came when I could quit.

Reminds me of the time when I owned a piece of land in Wilson County, Tennessee. I was out there one weekend cutting brush when two old guys drove up and asked me if I'd seen any stray calves. No, I said, I hadn't.

They were standing there watching me work, using what tools I had with me to do what I felt like doing right then, and finally one of them said, "Ain't making much progress clearing out that brush, are you?"

I stopped working and stood there looking at the pair of them for a few seconds. "Well," I said. "I figure farming ought to be like making love. It's not how fast you get it done as much as it's how much fun you have doing it!"

They looked at me, looked at each other, then looked back at me and each slapped his leg and burst out laughing. I went back to work but I could hear them still laughing as they drove away.

Geezer Gold
ALTERNATE MEANINGS OF MY FAVORITE WORDS

LIFE: activity, animation, effervescence, energy, sparkle, spirit, sprightliness, verve, vigor, performance

LOVE: adoration, affair, affection, amour, ardor, attachment, devotion, fondness, infatuation, passion, desire

HEALTH: robust, vigorous, dynamic, energetic, lively, red-blooded

HAPPINESS: bliss, contentment, euphoria, rapture, tranquility

PEACE: accord, agreement, concord, order, pacification, reconciliation

PROSPERITY: abundance, affluence, ease, thriving, well-being

> To take what there is, and use it, without waiting forever in vain for the preconceived—to dig deep into the actual and get something out of that—this doubtless is the right way to live.
> —Henry James

Self-Reliance; Not Self-Sufficiency

The secret of enjoying life through back-to-the-land country living before or after retirement is self-reliance. Not self-sufficiency, mind you. Because self-sufficiency implies that you have everything you need, and that you can get along without anyone or anything else. But no man is an island, and though it can be fun to figure out how to do everything safely on your own, there's no harm in accepting help when it's available.

I put the self-reliance method to a test one Saturday. It was the first week in October, and I needed to replace the wood-burning stove in my basement before winter.

The basement (which was dug under about 1/4 of the house and was only about 66 inches deep because members of the family who built the house were all short in stature) floods when it rains. When I took possession of the place (on a Saturday), the previous owner had (1) not told me that the basement flooded, and (2) had the electricity turned off (instead of just having the meter read).

Well, it rained, and when I arrived at the house on Sunday the basement was two feet deep in water. The stove sat on concrete blocks—but that wasn't quite high enough. There was a sump pump, but of course it wouldn't run without power—and anyway, the float switch was broken and you had to manually turn it on and off.

First, I tried using a garden hose to siphon the water out . . . but it wouldn't work—the outflow end of the hose can't be much higher than the inflow end. Since it was Sunday there was no place open where I could rent a pump. So I had to wait until Monday, then had the power turned on, and started the sump pump. And of course I repaired and later replaced the pump.

The water had rusted out the stove grate, the lower door hinge, and the ash pan—partially, I suspect, from previous such soakings. Possibly the grate could have been replaced, but it was hard to tell. Anyway I found another stove just like it at a fair price and decided I'd rather just start over.

But wood burning stoves are H-E-A-V-Y-! Getting the "new" one down the steep stairway wouldn't be too big a problem—gravity was in my favor. But first, how to get the old one up and out?

When I have to solve a problem like this, my first move is to think about it. I make it my business to pass by the site of any upcoming problem from time to time, and sort of imagine myself trying to solve it this way, and that way . . . and consider what would happen if my plan failed for one reason or another.

Step 2 is to see what I might have in my library by way of background information and also to watch for clues in my current reading. I've found that I often run across information about things I "need to know" just by keeping my eyes open and my mind receptive.

Also, I try to mention my dilemma to people I talk to on the off chance they've faced a similar situation themselves. If they have no practical experience, I find it best to disregard their advice.

Final step is to locate or obtain whatever tools (or helpers) my best plan indicates that I will (or might) need.

Thus when I was faced with hauling heavy buckets of clay out of the concrete tanks that stored my spring water, I didn't hesitate to buy a stout block and tackle. I thought it might help me with the tank cleaning, I knew it would be useful in stretching barbed wire when I got to my fence-building stage, and I now suspected it also would help move that stove up those basement steps.

And it did. I had a flat nylon tow strap (bought in case my old pickup broke down and I'd need to pull it home), so I wrapped the strap around the stove a couple of times. The block and tackle was hooked to my pickup truck's frame, parked at the top of the outdoor stairway, in gear, brakes set, and wheels chocked.

I laid some short 2x4s on the steps to serve as skids (would have used longer ones but didn't have any) and slowly but surely pushed on the stove while pulling on the block and tackle rope. So, in short, easy stages I moved the darn thing up the stairs—taking care not to stand where the stove might crush me should it break loose.

How did I get the new one down? A couple of strong young men stopped by to inspect something I had for sale. When I asked them if they'd help me with the stove, they picked it up and carried it down. I stood by and showed them where to set it.

Accepting this kind of help is not a violation of my "self-reliance code" but surely would be if I had claimed to be self-sufficient!

Geezer Gold

"The worst thing one can do is not to try, to be aware of what one wants and not give in to it, to spend years in silent hurt wondering if something could have materialized—and never knowing."—David S. Viscott

"Let your boat of life be light, packed with only what you need—a homely home, and simple pleasures, one or two friends worth the name, someone to love and someone to love you, a cat, a dog, a pipe or two, enough to eat and enough to wear, and a little more than enough to drink, for thirst is a dangerous thing."—Jerome Klapka Jerome (quoted in a book on simplifying your life)

"As to salvation and all that. . . . The greatest teachers, the true healers, I would say, have always insisted that they can only point the way. The Buddha went so far as to say: 'Believe nothing, no matter where you read it or who has said it, not even if I have said it, unless it agrees with your own reason and your own common sense.' The great ones do not set up offices, charge fees, or write books. Wisdom is silent, and the most effective propaganda for truth is the force of personal example. . . . The great ones are indifferent, in the profoundest sense. They don't ask you to believe; they electrify you by their behavior. They are the awakeners. What you do with your petty life is only of concern to you, they seem to say. In short, their only purpose here on earth is to inspire. And what more can one ask of a human being than that?"—As quoted by Henry Miller in *Sexus* (You may want to re-read the last paragraph.)

> All slang is metaphor, and all metaphor is poetry.
> G. K. Chesterton: *The Defendant, A Defense of Slang*

An Almost True Story

When she came through the door, right then I could see
She was the kind of a woman I'd want next to me.
But the bar wasn't crowded, mostly just men
Who were drinking, talking, looking for women.

She looked us all over and then she sat down
Right next to me as I ordered a round.
So I told the bartender, casual, I think,
Bring this young lady what she wants to drink.

She thanked me, and ordered tonic and gin
And as she sipped it, I knew she'd begin
To tell me her story, if she had one to tell;
One look in her eyes, you saw she'd known hell.

I'm country raised, she said, one daughter of seven
So I thought that the city would be like heaven.
But after these years of trying to earn
My own living here, I'm going to return.

Go back? I asked, and took a sip of my drink.
Be a child again? Is that what you think?

She looked down, then answered. No, those days are gone
But my granddad just died and left me his farm.

I'm blessed with beauty and I guess that's all right
But since living in the city I'm afraid of the night.
The next words she whispered, almost a moan:
My problem, she said, is I can't sleep alone.

And you, she went on, look like a man of the soil;
One who will work hard, stand up to the toil
Of planting the crops, and when harvest is done
I'll bet you know how to have us some fun!

So we left there together, drove home to her farm
And we're living there now, and building a new barn.
If you're a man alone, here's advice you might use:
Don't hurt to go drinking with manure on your shoes.

> One impulse from the vernal wood
> May teach you more of man,
> Of moral evil and of good
> Than all the sages can.
> —William Wordsworth

Night Sounds in the Country

There is one big difference between living in the city and living in the country. When you hear a "funny noise" somewhere in the house while living in the country, there's no way you can explain it away by making yourself believe that you or your spouse really didn't hear what you thought you heard.

For example, if there is a noise outside your window after midnight in the country, you darned sure know that it is made by someone or some thing that doesn't belong there. In the city, you can at least try to reassure yourself—or your nervous spouse—that the footsteps were made by someone visiting the house next door.

Same thing with all the noises that a country house makes at night. Let's say that you hear an electric motor running in your basement. If you have no basement, or if you do but there are no electric motors hooked up down there, you'd better start checking it out. It's possible that a swarm of bumblebees has decided to raise families under your floorboards, or something.

Another sound—early morning, this time—had me baffled for a time. After new neighbors moved into what had been a vacant house about a quarter-mile down the road, I started waking up about dawn every day, summer and winter. I knew it wasn't me, because I've never had any trouble sleeping late when I had no reason to rise early. Finally it occurred to me that my new neighbors had chickens! And the roosters were crowing every day to greet the crack of dawn!

Strangely, I never heard the roosters when I was awakened. But after it occurred to me that must be what was happening, I then started to hear the roosters crow. And, would you believe it, after I knew they were the cause, I no longer was awakened by their early get-up calls?

Lots of people who live in the country leave their giant yard lights burning all night. I had two—one close to the house that wasn't hooked up, and another installed by the previous owner a good distance away in the pasture where it did absolutely no good. Maybe it was an experiment to see if he could encourage his cows to graze at night. I'm told that lights in the hen house increase egg production by keeping the chickens awake and eating all night.

I could not decide whether to continue leaving my yard lights turned off or not. One theory might be that no one will risk fooling around a farmstead when an outdoor light is on. But then I suspected that anyone up to no good wouldn't even know I lived there if the lights were left off. As usual, the right course of action probably was somewhere in between. Buy one of those motion-activated light switches.

But that would violate the primary rule of successful farming: Don't spend any money!

ON THE ROAD AGAIN

" For my part, I travel not to go anywhere, but to go.
I travel for travel's sake.
The great affair is to move. "

Robert Louis Stevenson: *Travels with a Donkey*

Geezer Goof-Offs

I'm not assertive, Or I'd tell you direct
If we can't make love, You can go to heck.

I have but one heart, And if I had two
I'd take one out, And sell it to you.

Macho I'm not, Nor am I the other.
But if you're busy tonight, Could I take out your mother?

I wandered all alone Until you entered my life.
If I wasn't married, I'd make you my wife.

Being a true friend Is an art you've not mastered
And that's why we call you A really rotten bastard

Women's lib has changed A whole lot of things
If you want to get married, You buy the rings.

Each Saturday night I face this decision:
Read a good book. Or watch television.

> He that travelleth into a country before he hath some
> entrance into the language goeth to school and
> not to travel.
> —Francis Bacon: *Of Travel*

A Stranger in a Strange Land

I am living in France as I write these words, but this happened on my first visit there a few years ago. I flew into the Orly Airport at Paris, clutching instructions of how to take the metro to the train station. There I would board a high-speed train to Tours, home of Danyele Gallet, a French woman with whom I had corresponded as an international pen pal for some time and who had invited me to come for a visit.

But the plane arrived late, and I doubted my ability to make the necessary intermediate station and track changes on the subway, so I decided to splurge and take a taxi instead. I noticed that the line of cars with drivers obviously waiting for passengers did not have the usual "taxi" light on the roof, but, after all, I was in France.

So I approached the first driver and asked the fare to the train station. He quoted a figure in francs that amounted to about $60. I asked the next driver, and his answer was the same. So I took the first car—and later learned that I had engaged what is called a "limousine" though it looked like an ordinary car to me, but was not the smaller gas-saving vehicles that Europeans prefer due to the tax-induced high cost of gasoline there.

No problems buying my ticket to Tours—but then which of the 30-some tracks was mine? The ticket didn't say. I asked a man in a railroad uniform, and he just shrugged his shoulders and went about his business. Then I realized I needed to visit the men's room. And nowhere in the busy station could I see any sign that resembled the familiar man/woman symbols.

So, as I was standing there with a puzzled look on my face, another, older man stopped, apparently to try to help me. But I couldn't remember the French word for "bathroom." My little pocket translator was no help. So I began using body language, holding one leg over the other, and pointing to the appropriate section of my body.

The man gave me a disgusted look, and walked quickly away. By that time, my train had departed, so I returned to the ticket counter where I found a cashier who spoke some English. She exchanged my expired ticket for another one on the next train, told me to look at the huge overhead listing of destinations, departure times, and track numbers.

A men's room? Oh, she said, look for a sign that says "VC." I did. But only located one which said "WC," and immediately I realized that, like the Germans, the French pronounce "W" as we do "V" and vice versa. Or "wice wersa," I suppose it would be.

Later, I told my friend in Tours of my experience with the man who gave me the look of disgust as he walked away.

"Oh," she laughed, "he thought you were gay; and that you were propositioning him!"

I've told the story often to illustrate the difficulties of communicating effectively. And, no doubt, there is in Paris an older man who also has told the story frequently, probably to illustrate that it is the Americans, not the French, who are truly decadent.

> The French will only be united under the threat of danger. Nobody can simply bring together a country that has 265 kinds of cheese.
> —Charles de Gaulle

Life in a Small French Village

Fontaine (the word means "fountain") is one of many small country villages in the Department of Eure et Loir, just west and a bit south of Paris, near Chartres. Usually, two or three villages are joined for purposes of local government and our town hall is in nearby Ouerre (pronounced "where").

This is an area of farms, and the people who own the farmland do not want to "waste" it by building their houses, barns, etc., on an individual area of land. There are four farms headquartered in Fontaine. The farmers use large tractors and equipment, so not many employees are needed. Thus the additional houses—and new ones are always being added—are occupied by people employed nearby, by those who are retired, with a few Paris weekenders.

Like gasoline, electricity and bottled gas are relatively expensive in France, so many if not most houses also have a fireplace. Wood, however, also is expensive unless you have a woodlot. You don't see many big trees—even fewer since a terrible windstorm a few years ago.

Weekly trash pick up is provided, and recycling is encouraged. Which is not to say that all French people refrain from tossing trash out of their cars or utilizing illegal "dumps." Unfortunately.

Since even the brief summer temperatures hover around 70 degrees, air conditioning is uncommon. And every house is surrounded by a wire fence or, more frequently, mortared rock or concrete walls. Most lots also have tall hedges for added privacy, and nearly every house has a sign on the front gate (locked each night) that warns of a guard dog ("garde chien").

The dogs are zealous in protecting their turf, barking ferociously at passersby. Seldom would you see a dog—or a cat—loose on the streets. Nor do I often see a resident on my daily bike rides.

Nearly all roads between villages are blacktopped, but unless traffic is heavy on that route, most are only one lane wide—so when two cars meet, both must slow down and put one set of wheels on the grass shoulder. Otherwise, French drivers seem to drive as fast as possible, whenever possible.

Road signs at each village list the distance (in kilometers) to the next village or two, but seldom is there a sign telling you that you are on the right road to the nearest city. And, some of the country roads are not shown on highway maps. Apparently, the theory is that if you are going somewhere, you should already know how to get there!

But the maps do include a valuable feature for bike-riders: hills and the degree of slope. Makes it easy to select a route that requires less heavy pedaling. The French like to dress "correctly" for every endeavor; thus, Sunday cyclists travel in flocks, each dressed in those tight-fitting outfits favored by professional racers.

> "The struggle between good and evil takes place not
> so much between people as within them."
> Norman Cousins: *Saturday Review*, 1979

I Have Met the Universe, and It Is Us

After I had assembled all the parts of this little book, and put them into sections and chapters, I realized that I had not fully developed the title that I had finally selected for it. My first working title, by the way, was stolen from Ziggy, the comic page character:

"A Life Well-Lived; or I Always Was Afraid It Would Turn Out This Way."

Fortunately, better minds prevailed upon me to abandon that idea, and in due course the "geezer" approach beckoned and was recognized and allowed to remain. For, I'm sure, to the younger people to whom my tales are addressed, anyone over 50 surely must be in the geezer class. And I, most certainly, am over 50!

But let us discuss the Universe. Or, put it this way, I have researched the Universe and it is us. And we are it. For, truth to tell, each of us walks around in a body that's nothing more than a collection of quarks and other sub-atomic particles, organized into a body, which consists of a mind, a spiritual component, and the collection of cells that gives it all a form.

We create our reality, you know. Most people reject that idea, and probably because they don't want to take responsibility for who and what they are. But quantum physics tells us that it is true: we are what we will ourselves to be; and further, what we "see" is based on how evolution and our socialization as infants has hardwired our mind to interpret what our senses perceive.

Thus, as accumulations of energy, that, in its alter ego form become "matter," each of us may be in constant connection with every other particle/wave in the entire universe. And, in my opinion and that of many others much more informed than I am, this connection exists through what we call our subconscious mind. Some call it "our higher self." Others call it "God." Doesn't really matter what we call it: A rose by any other name would smell as sweet, according to Shakespeare. My opinion is our whole obsession with naming everything is really our futile attempt to exert our power over that thing.

We "see" or experience the reality of our universe in the way our minds have been socialized to see it—partially through our genetic coding, but also through how we experience the reality we find when we are born. Think of it this way: A computer chip "knows" only 1's and 0's, which are transformed by a program into letters, numbers, and pictures. Thus our brains are programmed to present the 1's and 0's of the universe as a reality that matches our brain's ability to discern it.

Going a step beyond, our most reliable connection to "everything" is through our heart—that is, through our emotions, or feelings. And I'm not talking just about "lust" here, though of course that is a part of it.

The unfortunate "joke" the universe plays on us is that we tend to seek the material thing. Even in our constant searches for new or renewed relationships, we seem to look for the tangible evidence of the relationship instead of seeking the intangible emotion that we actually want. Which is the "feeling" that comes with success. Because the feeling IS the success.

Marketing professionals know this, though they may fail to

apply it to their own lives. Thus: "Sell the sizzle and not the steak," as one exceptional salesman exhorted. Or, "sell the benefits and not the features," as I was often advised during my ad-writing days.

Works both ways. Look for the feeling, not for the object, be it human or inanimate. Concern yourself with acquiring the heart's currency. Do these things, and your storehouse of satisfactions will far exceed the gold in Fort Knox!

Love, Life, Health, Happiness, Peace, and Prosperity. To me, these are the most worthy goals of a life well lived.

Geezer Garden

Lyrics to an old country song (country, because I said so, and I wrote it—words and music. Old, because I wrote it maybe 30 years ago. It was accepted by a publisher in Nashville, never recorded, but was sung once in public, out of tune, by a semi-professional singer):

* * *

In a big town restaurant, he drinks his coffee slow
And thinks about the time he has and the places he won't go
Remembering that his yesterdays are like the days before
And doubting if tomorrow is still worth his waiting for

He watches the other customers who seldom seem to speak
Except to tell the waitress of the things they want to eat
Her face brings memories to his mind of one who was his wife
And how he's missed her every day since sadness filled his life

(chorus)
And he's wonderin', what he's doing there
And who will know the who or what or why
He can't realize, that if he is alive
Why the world's decided not to care

He pays his check with a dollar bill and walks slowly to the door
Deciding though the food was fine he won't eat there anymore
Then standing on the sidewalk he sees traffic moving by
And checks his watch against the clock and decides it's time to die
Yes, he checks his watch against the clock and decides it's time to die.

An Afterword

One of the best pieces of advice I can give you is this:

Learn to listen to your heart.

Make it an everyday practice to ask for that which you most desire . . . not by spelling out exactly what you want, but by imagining how you will *feel* when you get it. As the French mathematician and philosopher Pascal said: "The heart has reasons that reason will never know."

And, I'd like also to pass along some advice from Joan Borysenko, Ph.D., who was director of Harvard Medical School's Mind/Body Clinic when she wrote *Minding the Body, Mending the Mind*. Published in 1987 by Addison-Wesley, it's a book I highly recommend. The following 12 worthwhile suggestions are more fully explained in her book.

You cannot control the external circumstances of your life, but you can control your reactions to them.

Optimal health is the product of both physical and mental factors.

You could think of yourself as healthy.

Things change. Change is the only constant in life.

Your beliefs are incredibly powerful.

The only escape from stress, fear, and doubt is to confront them directly and see them for what they are.

Emotions fall into two broad categories, fear and love.

Would you rather be right or would you rather experience peace? (I liked this one so much that I added it to my Top Five Rules. dg)

Accept yourself as you are.

Practice forgiveness (letting go).

Stay open to life's teachings.

Be patient. Patience means mindful awareness.

(THE END)

Geezer Gruel

Along the way, [Patrick] Marber, who directs the play ("Closer") with less sureness of rhythm than he writes with, adds some original touches to the landscape of desire, including some very memorable girl talk about guys.

"We [women] arrive with our baggage and for a while they [men] are brilliant, they're baggage handlers," says the photographer to the lap dancer. "We say, 'Where's your baggage?' They deny all knowledge of it, they're in love, they have none." She continues, "Then, just as you're relaxing, a great big juggernaut arrives . . . with their baggage. It got held up. The greatest myth men have about women is that we over pack.."—*New Yorker* magazine, July 21, 1997, in a review

"In your amours you should prefer old women to young ones. They are so grateful."—Ben Franklin: letter to a young man June 25, 1745

Geezer Glimpses

I am only one,
But still I am one.
I cannot do everything,
But still I can do something;
And because I cannot do everything
I will not refuse to do the something that I can do.
—Edward Everett Hale, for the Lend-a-Hand Society

What men call gallantry, and gods adultery,
Is much more common where the climate's sultry.
—Byron: *Don Juan*